IPSWICH TOWN FC

The 1960s, from Ramsey to Robson

TERRY HUNT

EAST ANGLIAN
DAILY TIMES

EveningStar

IPSWICH TOWN FC
The 1960s, from Ramsey to Robson

TERRY HUNT

DB
PUBLISHING

First published in Great Britain in 2009 by
The Breedon Books Publishing Company Limited
Breedon House, 3 The Parker Centre,
Derby, DE21 4SZ.

This paperback edition published in Great Britain in 2014 by DB Publishing,
an imprint of JMD Media Ltd

ISBN 978-1-78091-392-6

Printed and bound in the UK by Copytech (UK) Ltd Peterborough

Contents

Dedication

This book is dedicated to the memory of Ipswich Town's greatest-ever managers, Sir Alf Ramsey and Sir Bobby Robson.

Arguments will continue for all time over whose achievement was the greater: was it Sir Alf winning the First Division Championship in 1962 with a team branded as no-hopers; or was it Sir Bobby's decade of glory in the 1970s and early 1980s, during which time he won the FA Cup, and the UEFA Cup, and came so agonisingly close to winning the League?

For me, their achievements cannot be separated. Their successes, and their legacies, have played a huge part in making Ipswich Town Football Club what it is today. This book spans the era between Sir Alf's triumphs and Sir Bobby's arrival. There are a few difficult days in between!

A donation from the proceeds of this book will be made to the Sir Bobby Robson Foundation, to aid research into cancer.

Foreword

It was my childhood friend Paul Scarff who first introduced me to Ipswich Town. The date was Saturday 27 April 1968, and Ipswich were playing Second Division promotion rivals Queen's Park Rangers. The game ended 2–2, and Town were promoted a few weeks later. From then on, I was hooked.

In the four decades and a bit since, I've joined thousands of other Town fans on a roller-coaster ride. There were the highs of the Robson years, when impossible dreams came true. Who would have imagined that Ipswich Town would win the FA Cup, or capture the UEFA Cup? Such triumphs were beyond my wildest dreams when I started supporting 'The Town'. More recently, there was the thrilling Play-off victory at Wembley in 2000.

Inevitably, there have also been several lows. The agony of three relegations, and some very dull seasons under John Duncan. The last season of Jim Magilton's managerial reign wasn't particularly memorable, either.

This book looks back to the black-and-white days of the 1960s. It contains more than 300 photographs, mostly from the unrivalled archive we have here at the *East Anglian Daily Times* and *Evening Star*. Many of these fascinating pictures have never before been published.

They capture a decade which began with Ramsey's unsung, unfancied team winning promotion to the First Division and then, astonishingly, becoming champions of England at their first attempt. It also covers the short-lived and disastrous reign of Jackie Milburn, the rebuilding process under Bill McGarry and the arrival of a young Bobby Robson. There are stars such as Ray Crawford, Bill Baxter, Mick Mills and Colin Viljoen. There are also other players who most people have forgotten even existed!

Above all, I hope the book has captured the essence of Ipswich Town in the 1960s. It was an era before players earned big money, when they were grateful to be given a turkey at Christmas, or a juicy steak. It was a decade of muddy pitches, a slightly ramshackle Portman Road and fans wearing collars and ties and waving rattles.

I hope you enjoy the memories.

Terry Hunt

1960–61: Heading for glory

After three frankly average seasons in Division Two, Ipswich Town were not expected to be anything more than a mid-table side in 1960–61. But they proved the pundits wrong. Thanks mainly to the astonishing goalscoring feats of twin strikers Ray Crawford and Ted Phillips, Town stormed to the Division Two Championship and were heading for top-flight football for the first time in the club's history.

Ipswich scored no fewer than 100 League goals that season, with Crawford (40) and Phillips (30) scoring an incredible 70 between them. A 13-match unbeaten run from December to April sealed Town's promotion, and they grabbed the Division Two title by one point from Sheffield United. That season saw Alf Ramsey make three significant signings: Bill Baxter, John Compton, and Roy Stephenson. They were all to play their part in the incredible story that was about to unfold.

Division Two final position: 1st.
FA Cup: Third Round.
League Cup: First Round.

The architect of Ipswich Town's success in the early 1960s, manager Alf Ramsey is pictured in the spartan surrounding of his office. As usual, he seems rather ill at ease when facing a camera. In public, Ramsey was withdrawn, sometimes difficult, but just about everyone who played for him, whether for Ipswich Town or England, idolises the man.

Great things were just around the corner. The Ipswich Town squad for 1960–61 lines up for the camera. After finishing mid-table in Division Two the previous season, nothing much was expected from Town. But the pundits were to be proved very, very wrong.

The Ipswich Town directors' box in the late 1950s or early 1960s. The Cobbold brothers, Mr John and Mr Patrick, are in the front row among a rather sombre-looking lot.

Ipswich Town football fans, 1960s style. These old men were probably survivors of World War One, and they deserved their seats. Many of them had probably been watching Town since the amateur days.

Ipswich Town fans enjoyed a very happy Christmas in 1960, when their promotion-chasing side beat Norwich twice in the course of two days. On Boxing Day Ipswich won 3–0 at Carrow Road, with Crawford scoring twice and Phillips once. The following day, at Portman Road, Ipswich ran out 4–2 winners, with Crawford getting two more and Phillips scoring from the penalty spot, and Doug Millward getting the other. The picture shows action from the Portman Road game, with Crawford helping himself to another Christmas present from the Canaries. Town ended the season as Division Two champions, while Norwich finished a respectable fourth.

Going to the football? Better put on a collar and tie! The Portman Road faithful all seem to have put on their Sunday best for this game in the early 1960s. Collar and ties abound, and only the daring have 'dressed down' in open-neck shirts!

Bizarre: The famous Ipswich Town Football Club 'missing man' picture, taken in April 1961, with a gap left for the absent Bill Baxter to be 'pasted in' later. Baxter was away on National Service.

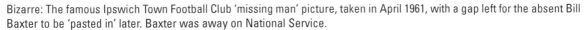

The crowd scenes on the Cornhill in Ipswich in 1961 as fans celebrate Ipswich reaching the First Division for the first time. A year later, the fans would be back and celebrating Robson again.

1961–62: The most unlikely champions

Unsung, unfancied, and surely heading straight back to Division Two. Well, that is what everyone thought as Alf Ramsey's side of assorted cast-offs and misfits lined up in a division bristling with superstar teams such as Spurs and Burnley. A 0–0 draw and two defeats in the first three games seemed to confirm everything the so-called experts were predicting.

But a 6–2 win over Burnley in the next game made everyone sit up and take notice, and the rest, as they say, is history. Opposition defences simply could not cope with Ramsey's tactical masterstroke of withdrawing wingers Roy Stephenson and Jimmy 'Sticks' Leadbetter, who supplied the ammunition for strikers Crawford and Phillips.

The dynamic duo ran riot, with Crawford scoring 33 League goals and Phillips 28. The goals were not exactly shared around in those days: of Town's 93 League goals, 90 came from the forward line of Stephenson, Moran, Crawford, Phillips and Leadbetter. Elsworthy's two and an own-goal were the only gatecrashers at this private party!

Town clinched the Division One title on the last day of the season with a 2–0 win over Aston Villa. Cue one almighty celebration!

Division One final position: Champions.

FA Cup: Fourth Round.

League Cup: Fourth Round.

The most unlikely League champions? Almost certainly. This was the line up that won the Division One title, against all the odds, in 1961–62. They owed their triumph to a combination of Alf Ramsey's tactical genius and extraordinary good fortune with injuries. Larry Carberry, Doug Moran and Andy Nelson played every game, Ray Crawford, John Elsworthy, Jimmy Leadbetter and Roy Stephenson each missed one game, Bill Baxter and Ted Phillips were out for two games each, John Compton missed three, while Roy Bailey was injured for five matches. Town used only 16 players in League games and, apart from the established first XI, the player to make the most appearances was reserve 'keeper Wilf Hall, with the grand total of five.

It was August 1961, and a new challenge was in store. Town players Ken Malcolm, Andy Nelson, Roy Bailey, Ted Phillips and Roy 'Rocky' Stephenson are pictured outside their hotel in Bolton after arriving for the first Division One game in Ipswich Town's history. A goalless draw was a satisfactory enough start, but it did nothing to stop the doom merchants who forecast that Town would go straight back down from where they had come. They were wrong by the length of a division!

The Town players were obviously a target for young autograph hunters as they arrived in Bolton for their first taste of Division One football in August 1961. Most pundits thought they would do well just to stay up. Nine months later, all the so-called experts were eating their words.

Town make their First Division debut in August 1961. A goalless draw gave little hint of the triumphs which were to follow.

A glimpse of Town's first taste of the big-time. Ipswich made their bow in the First Division on 19 August 1961 with a game at Bolton. They made a respectable start, drawing 0–0, but there was no hint of the fireworks to come as the season progressed. Here, Town snuff out another Bolton attack.

An historic day at Portman Road. Town played their fourth game in Division One on 29 August 1961, having not recorded a victory in the division. They have not yet recorded a victory. But that wrong was righted in some style. Against one of the best teams in the League, Ipswich won 6–2 with goals from Crawford (two), Stephenson, Moran, Phillips and Leadbetter – the complete forward line on target. This was the first sign that perhaps little Ipswich were going to be rather more than whipping boys. In the picture, Crawford challenges Burnley 'keeper Blacklaw in typically robust fashion.

All smiles for the camera in September 1961, as the crowd at Portman Road waits for Town to take on Fulham. There were fewer smiles at the end of the game, as Fulham won 4–2, despite Ray Crawford's two goals. Little did they know, these fans were watching history in the making. At the end of the season Town were top of the pile.

One of the Town goals in a 4–2 win over West Ham in October 1961. Both Crawford and Phillips scored twice. The young West Ham number four, on the right of the picture, is Geoff Hurst, who played at wing-half that day. He was later converted into a striker, with some success, apparently...

A sight to make opposing defences quake. The deadly duo of Crawford and Phillips, who terrorised defenders and goalkeepers in the late 1950s and early 1960s.

Crawford shoots, and scores. It was a very familiar sight for Town fans in the 1960s. Having signed from Portsmouth in 1958, Crawford went on to be Town's all-time top goalscorer in two highly successful spells.

The power of Ted Phillips's penalty kicks was legendary – some said 'keepers deliberately dived the wrong way. The speeding ball has become a mere blur in this picture.

Five of the Ipswich Town heroes who took the club on an incredible journey from apparent no-hopers to the First Division Championship in 1962. From the left: Roy Bailey, Larry Carberry, Andy Nelson, John Elsworthy, and John Compton.

Smiles from Town stalwarts: From the left: Ken Malcolm, Jimmy Leadbetter and Bill Baxter. Ken Malcolm had been a regular for six seasons, but he lost his place to John Compton in the 1961–62 Championship-winning year, making only three appearances. Both Leadbetter and Baxter played rather more pivotal roles.

Roy 'Rocky' Stephenson, who played such an integral part in Ipswich winning the League Championship in 1962.

Alf Ramsey takes a call in his less-than-luxurious Portman Road office. The items on his desk are interesting: a copy of the now defunct *Daily Dispatch*, and some de-icer. Was the de-icer to make sure his car started on frosty days or, as some less-than-charitable wags might suggest, to thaw out his less-than-warm public image? To be fair, those who worked closely with Ramsey – in particular his Ipswich and England players – saw a very different side to the great man.

A little-remembered fact about the otherwise triumphant 1961–62 season was the name of the team that knocked Town out of the FA Cup at the fourth-round stage. Yes, it was Norwich City. The teams drew 1–1 at Carrow Road, in front of 39,890, but Town lost the replay at Portman Road 2–1. Still, it left them free to concentrate on the League! Here, Andy Nelson leads out his team for the first game. Bearing in mind this was 27 January, the chap on the left holding the umbrella seems a little under-dressed!

It's the championship season, but fans of Norwich City had a moment of glory at Town's expense in the FA Cup. After a 1–1 draw at Carrow Road, Town lost 2–1 in the fourth-round replay at Portman Road. Terry Allcock scored both the Canaries' goals, including a late winner. This picture shows stalwarts Andy Nelson and John Elsworthy in action.

The slightly odd-looking Norwich mascot gently teasing Ipswich fans before the FA Cup fourth-round match at Carrow Road in January 1962. The visiting supporters seem to be taking it with good humour.

It really is a question of 'spot the ball' as Town attack the Norwich goal in the Fourth Round FA Cup tie at Carrow Road in January 1962. Jimmy Leadbetter's goal gave Town a draw, but Norwich won the replay at Portman Road 2–1.

In February 1962 Everton were the latest members of English football's elite to come a cropper at Portman Road. Having beaten Town 5–2 at Goodison Park earlier in the season, the Toffees (as they were called then) were thrashed 4–0 in the away game, with Town's goalscorers Crawford, Phillips, Moran and Elsworthy. Here is one of the goals, with Doug Moran in the thick of the action.

A rare sight indeed – a headed goal from Jimmy Leadbetter. This was 3 March 1962, and Town thrashed Sheffield United 4–0, with other goals coming from Crawford (two) and Moran. This was part of an unbeaten 10-match run as the triumphant 1961–62 season built to a climax.

Roy Bailey diving for the camera. Bailey was Town's 'keeper through the Ramsey glory years. His son, Gary, has less happy memories of Portman Road, where he conceded six goals in 1980. Mind you, he also saved three penalties in the same game! The background to this picture shows just how homespun Portman Road remained, even when the team was the best in the land.

Jimmy Leadbetter never looked like a finely honed athlete. But what a crucial role 'Sticks' played in Ramsey's tactical masterplan that took the footballing nation completely by surprise. This photo was taken during a hot pre-season training session, if the state of Jimmy's shirt is anything to go by.

A portrait of a young John Cobbold, part of the dynasty who ran the football club for so many decades. It was 'Mr John' who famously kept faith with Bobby Robson after fans called for his head during a League Cup defeat by a George Best-inspired Manchester United in 1971. Who owns the bike in the background of this picture? A fan, or a player?

'WAGS' 1960s-style. Sir Alf Ramsey's public personna was always notoriously frosty, especially with the 'gentlemen of the Press'. But there were occasions when he relaxed, such as this social gathering, where he is pictured with some of his players' wives.

Larry Carberry and John Compton – two of the unsung heroes of Ramsey's 1962 Championship-winning side.

'And this is a ball.' Trainer Jimmy Forsyth looks like he is going back to basics with reserve-team players in the early 1960s.

Big John Elsworthy first played for Town way back in 1949, but he emerged as a star performer more than a decade later as Ramsey's unsung heroes won the Division Two and Division One titles in successive seasons in the early 1960s. Quite how Big John failed to win a single senior Welsh cap remains a total mystery to those who watched him play.

Local boy Ted Phillips demonstrating his legendary shooting power to an admiring Ken Malcolm. Phillips teamed up with Ray Crawford to terrorise defences up and down the land. Legend has it that one of Ted's 'Thunderbolts' was so fierce that it broke the net. There are also tales of cowardly 'keepers diving out of the way of his spot-kicks.

Roy Stephenson, who was converted by Alf Ramsey from journeyman right-winger into provider of an avalanche of goals for Ray Crawford and Ted Phillips. Stephenson had had a long but relatively undistinguished career until joining Ipswich in 1960. Ramsey's tactical brilliance transformed him, and he and Leadbetter provided the ammunition for Crawford and Phillips to terrorise firstly Second Division defences, and then the best defenders in the land.

Alf Ramsey's capture of Ray Crawford from his home-town club Portsmouth was a masterstroke. Teamed up with Ted Phillips, Crawford became one of the most prolific strikers in England, firing Town to the Division One title in 1962. After leaving for Wolves and also having a spell at West Bromwich Albion, Bill McGarry brought Crawford back to Town, and he played a big part in their return to Division One in 1968. Crawford was still scoring goals in 1971, as mighty Leeds learned to their regret when Crawford sank them in the FA Cup at Layer Road. Crawford's 227 goals for Town is a record which will never be beaten.

Andy Nelson leading out the team for another game at Portman Road. Nelson was signed from West Ham in 1959, and proved to be one of Ramsey's many shrewd acquisitions.

This game against struggling Cardiff was played on 14 April 1962. Just two weeks later, Town were crowned champions. They disposed of Cardiff thanks to a Doug Moran goal. Note the rattles!

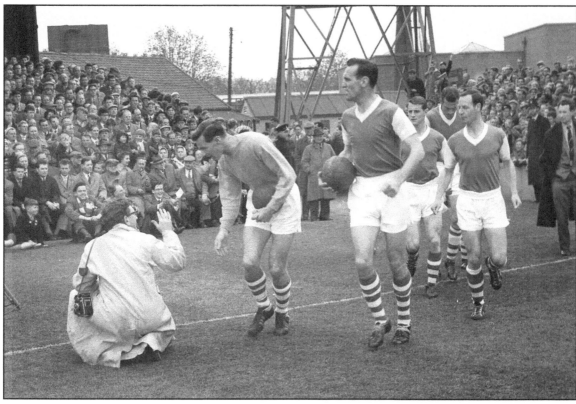

What was Roy Bailey saying to the photographer as the team ran on to the pitch at Portman Road? Knowing the capacity for fun in those far-off footballing days, the conversation was almost certainly friendly.

The Ipswich Town forward line which brought the Division One trophy to Portman Road for the one and only time – so far. From the left: Roy 'Rocky' Stephenson, Doug Moran, Ray Crawford, Ted Phillips and Jimmy Leadbetter. What would this line up be worth in today's transfer market?

A study of 'local boy made good' Ted Phillips. Ted, from Snape, had a mixed few years with Town in the 1950s, even being loaned out to Stowmarket for one season. It was when Ramsey teamed him up with the new arrival from Portsmouth, a certain Ray Crawford, that things really began to take off for Ted. Why did he not play for England?

Pitch invasions are nothing new. Excited youngsters run on to the pitch for a closer view of their Ipswich Town heroes.

This was the game when Town created history. Town beat visitors Aston Villa 2–0 to clinch the Division One crown. Here, Ray Crawford stretches to keep the ball in play. It was Crawford's two goals on that historic day which saw Town crowned as champions.

Action from the crucial, Championship-deciding game against Aston Villa at Portman Road in 1962. Here, a shot from Ted Phillips goes just wide much to the relief of Villa 'keeper Sims. Ray Crawford is in close attendance.

28 April 1962. The ball is on its way to the back of the net, thanks to Ray Crawford's diving header after John Elsworthy had hit the bar. The Aston Villa 'keeper, Sims, looks on helplessly. The referee, Mr Crawford (no relation!), looks on, apparently open-mouthed with admiration. Less than half an hour later, unfancied Ipswich were crowned League champions.

Some people are on the pitch, they think it's all over…It was just a few minutes later. Ray Crawford is mobbed after scoring both goals to beat Aston Villa in the final game of the 1961–62 season. Shortly afterwards, it was confirmed that Ipswich were the champions of England.

The end of a memorable season – but Ipswich Town and their fans do not yet know whether they have won the First Division title. As the players run off after the last game against Aston Villa, their achievement is not yet confirmed. They only had to wait a few minutes before the celebrations started in earnest.

Roy Bailey is the only Town player to keep his boots on as they line up to be interviewed by the BBC after the astonishing League Championship triumph in 1962.

Ipswich have just stunned the footballing world by winning the League Championship, but you would not know it from the stiff-upper-lip demeanour of Alf Ramsey and the Nice Man From the Beeb.

The TV reporter is momentarily distracted from his task of interviewing the new champions of England. Note Ramsey's hand in his pocket – a characteristic pose which would later be immortalised in his statue overlooking Portman Road, which was unveiled by his widow, Lady Victoria, and some of his 1962 League-winning side in August 2000.

The triumphant Town players being interviewed after clinching the Division One title in 1962.

Roy Bailey, John Elsworthy, Larry Carberry, Ted Phillips and Jimmy Leadbetter tell the man from the Beeb how they managed to shock the footballing nation by winning the Division One title in 1962 in their very first season in the top flight of English football.

Roy Bailey enjoys a drink as Town players celebrate their triumph in 1962. The dressing room looks rather crowded!

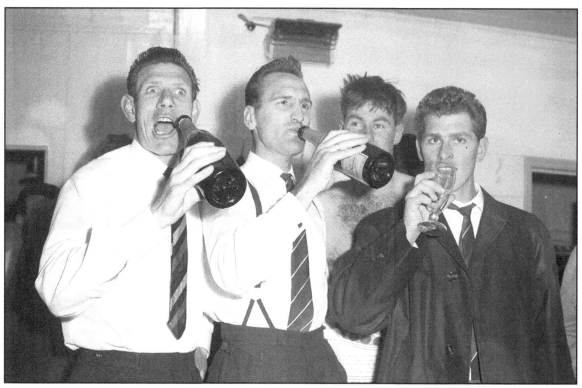

Ever the joker, Ted Phillips hams it up for the camera as serious celebrations get under way. Roy Bailey seems to be rather slow getting dressed!

The all-conquering Town team arrives on the traditional open-top bus in 1962, after astonishing the world of football – and probably themselves – by winning the First Division Championship.

We are the champions! The triumphant Town team arrives on the Cornhill in Ipswich in the traditional open-top bus to be greeted by thousands of adoring fans.

The amazing scenes on the Cornhill and Tavern Street, Ipswich, in 1962 as thousands of Ipswich Town fans wait to greet their heroes. In this photo, taken from the first floor of Grimwade's store, the thousands of supporters disappear into the far distance. These scenes would be repeated in 1978, when Town brought home the FA Cup.

A solitary policeman seems to be standing guard over thousands of fans celebrating Town's Division One Championship triumph in 1962. Some people are taking their lives in their hands by clambering out of the Sun Life windows to get a better view of their heroes.

Give us a wave: Ipswich Town players acknowledge their fans on the steps of Ipswich Town Hall in 1962, as the celebrations get underway.

Skipper Andy Nelson holds the First Division Championship trophy aloft as the Town players arrive on the Cornhill in Ipswich for the civic celebrations in 1962. The base of the trophy is in the safe hands of smiling 'keeper Roy Bailey.

The open-top bus carrying the newly crowned Division One champions arrives on the Cornhill in Ipswich. Bizarrely, the players have been joined in their celebrations by Miss Witch, the mascot of the Ipswich Witches speedway team.

A different view of the celebrations to mark Town winnning the 1961–62 League Championship. Taken from the first floor of Grimwades outfitters shop, this image shows the scene as the players pose with the Cup for the posse of photographers in front of Ipswich Town Hall.

Manager Alf Ramsey receiving an official gift from Ipswich Mayor Charlotte Green in 1962. Chairman John Cobbold looks faintly bored by proceedings.

Big John Elsworthy proudly showing the 1962 League Championship trophy to the fans. Elsworthy had played for Town since the late 1940s.

Smile for the camera: tactical genius and brilliant motivator of players, Alf Ramsey was never at his best when a camera was pointed in his direction. He proves the point here in this picture with Ipswich Mayor Charlotte Green at the celebrations in 1962.

The Ipswich Town mascot looks less than enthralled by chairman John Cobbold's speech during the celebrations after Town won the First Division Championship in 1962.

League champions Ipswich Town celebrate their 1962 triumph on the steps of Ipswich Town Hall.

Another party – Ted Phillips, Andy Nelson, Roy Bailey and Ray Crawford celebrating another footballing triumph. Ted seems to be concentrating on choosing his next drink.

Ted Phillips pictured in an unusually pensive mood during the celebrations for Ipswich winning the 1962 League Championship. Andy Nelson seems to be having a quiet word in Ted's ear, while also pictured are chairman John Cobbold, Roy Bailey and Ray Crawford. Just visible, far left, is Pat Godbold, who has served the club so loyally for many decades.

Steady on, chaps! Ipswich policemen are hard pressed to keep back the excited Town fans during the 1962 Championship celebrations.

'Go on, Alf, say something.' Most of the party-goers are looking expectantly at the Ipswich manager at this celebration – one of many during Ramsey's successful reign.

Extraordinary scenes as Ipswich fans celebrate their team's amazing League Championship triumph in 1962.

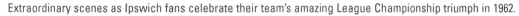

The Moet has been cracked open, and the Town players are getting stuck in. Yet another celebration from the amazing Ramsey era.

Dry old do, isn't it? The Town players – Andy Nelson, Ted Phillips, and John Compton – seem rather short of liquid refreshment as other guests happily help themselves during this celebration.

Don't drop me, lads! Andy Nelson does not look especially comfortable as he is hoisted skyward by John Elsworthy and Roy Bailey during the 1962 Championship celebrations. John Compton seems to be having a few problems lifting up the Town mascot as well. A fantastic celebration to end an incredible season.

1962–63: The slide begins

Having been taken by surprise by the 'Country Cousins' of Ipswich once, English football's elite was never going to fall for it again. The writing was on the wall from day one, when Spurs thrashed Town 5–1 in the Charity Shield. As well as being 'twigged' tactically, Town also had injuries to contend with as key players aged. The settled side of the previous season was a distant memory as fringe players were forced to cover for injured stars. Town especially missed the goalscoring feats of Phillips, who managed only nine League goals, although his striking partner Crawford maintained his form, scoring 25 in the League. For a while, Town looked in danger of being relegated, but improved results in the second half of the season saw them finish 17th.

One highlight was the club's first foray into European competition. Maltese part-timers Floriana were seen off 14–1 on aggregate in the preliminary round of the European Cup, before Town lost 4–2 on aggregate to European aristocrats AC Milan.

Division One final position: 17th.

FA Cup: Fourth Round.

European Cup: First Round.

Ipswich Town were champions of England – would they suffer from what has become known as 'second-season syndrome?' It was August 1962, and the first game of the 1962–63 season, with Town entertaining Blackburn. This game went quite well, a 3–3 draw with Ray Crawford scoring twice and Doug Moran getting the other. But it was to be the start of a difficult few years for Town.

Town beat Blackpool 5–2 at Portman Road in August 1962 at the start of the second season in Division One. It was one of the few highlights.

Everyone seemed to be having a jolly time as the teams took to the pitch for Ipswich Town versus Floriana of Malta in the European Cup, 1962. Ken Malcolm skippered the Ipswich team, deputising for Andy Nelson. At the end of the night, only the Ipswich players were still smiling – they won 10–0.

Over 25,000 turned out to watch Town's home debut in Europe. They beat Maltese side Floriana 10–0 in the preliminary round of the European Cup, 14–1 on aggregate, in September 1962. The first round proper was a different story, with Town going out 4–2 on aggregate to Italian giants AC Milan. It was Town's only venture into European's premier Cup competition – so far!

Roy Stephenson challenges for a cross against Wolves in September 1962. Despite goals from Doug Moran and Ray Crawford, Town lost this game 3–2. It was part of a run of nine games without a win which sank the reigning champions into relegation trouble.

Doug Moran, far left, celebrates his goal against Wolves in September 1962. Ted Phillips is also happy to see the ball cross the line. Unfortunately, Town ended up losing 3–2.

Simple pleasures. Mascots Ian Harvey and 'Swede' Herring, an Ipswich bus conductor, entertain the crowd before Town's first foray into Europe, against Maltese side Floriana in September 1962. The game was even better than the pre-match entertainment – Town won 10–0.

These fans were about to be treated to a thriller against Manchester United in November 1962. Town scored three times, through Bobby Blackwood (two) and Ray Crawford, but the Red Devils scored five, including four from a certain Denis Law.

On 1 December 1962 Town played a game which was to become the most notorious in English footballing history. The facts and figures are innocuous enough. Town beat Sheffield Wednesday 2–0 at Portman Road, with Ray Crawford scoring both goals. The result was very welcome for the Blues who, although they were reigning champions, were finding life difficult in their second top-flight season. In fact, this was only their fourth League win of the campaign. The scoreline would have been mildly surprising at the time, because Wednesday were a strong outfit, boasting a number of current England internationals. But it was certainly not a remarkable result. It was almost 18 months later that the game hit the national headlines – for all the wrong reasons. The *Sunday People* newspaper reported that three Wednesday players – Peter Swan, Tony Kay and David 'Bronco' Layne – had placed bets on their own side to lose the game. Their winnings amounted to the princely sum of £100 each. All three were subsequently convicted of fraud, jailed, and banned from football for life. In Swan's case, it robbed him of the chance of a World Cup-winner's medal. Many experts believed that he would have been England's centre-half in 1966, rather than Jack Charlton. Eventuallly, his life ban was lifted, and he played one final season for Wednesday in the early 1970s. The picture shows Swan (number five) and 'keeper Ron Springett sprawled on the Portman Road turf as Ray Crawford (also on the ground) scores one of the goals in English football's most infamous game.

Action from English football's most notorious game. John Elsworthy heads towards goal in the match against Sheffield Wednesday at Portman Road in December 1962. Ray Crawford (number nine) awaits developments, and Wednesday's England centre-half Peter Swan (number five) is on the far right.

The crowd in the West Stand at Portman Road (replaced two decades later by the Pioneer Stand) waiting for Town to take on Sheffield Wednesday in December 1962. Ray Crawford's two goals saw Ipswich grab a very welcome 2–0 win. Little did these fans realise that the game they were watching was to become the most infamous in English footballing history.

Things had turned rather sour for Town fans by the time this picture was taken at the game against Arsenal at Portman Road in March 1963. Town were struggling near the bottom of the First Division, and the previous year's title glory was a fast-fading memory. Ipswich did at least manage a 1–1 draw in this game, thanks to a Ted Phillips penalty. Terry Neill, Joe Baker (brother of future Ipswich striker Gerry) and George Eastham were among the Arsenal players.

Town drew this home game against Leyton Orient 1–1 in April 1963, thanks to Doug Moran's goal. It was not a great result against the team destined to finish rock bottom of the First Division that season, but a point at least kept Ipswich's hopes of avoiding relegation alive. They would eventually finish sixth from bottom, four points away from the drop. It was only a stay of execution, however.

Another game, another Ray Crawford goal? Wrong this time, actually – the camera does lie on occasions! In actual fact, it was the less celebrated Doug Moran who netted Town's goal in this game against Leyton Orient in April 1963, clinching a much-needed point and edging Ipswich further away from trouble. They eventually escaped relegation by four points.

The Portman Road crowd at the game against Burnley in April 1963. Town were struggling to stay in the top division, and the 2–1 win over the visitors from Lancashire was very welcome. Crawford and Phillips scored the goals. Crawford remained as prolific as ever, scoring 25 League goals, but Phillips struggled, netting only nine times.

1963–64: 'Too nice to be a manager'

The writing had been on the wall in the previous season, as Town flirted with relegation. This time round, there was no saving themselves. Ramsey had gone to the England job, and Newcastle legend 'Wor Jackie' Milburn had taken his place. Nice guy Milburn had no chance. He inherited an ageing squad from Ramsey, and then sold off his prize asset, Ray Crawford, just six games into the season. His forays into the transfer market, mainly in Scotland, were largely unsuccessful, and Town's season went from bad to worse.

They finished bottom of Division One, conceding no fewer than 121 goals. Humiliating defeats included a record 10–1 at Fulham, 9–1 at Stoke, 7–2 at home to Manchester United, 6–0 at Bolton and Liverpool, and 6–3 at Spurs. The most often used quote about the hapless Milburn was that he was 'far too nice a man to be a football manager.' Town's three-season First Division adventure was over – for the time being.

Division One final position: 22nd.

FA Cup: Fourth Round.

League Cup: Second Round.

Ipswich players and officials leaving Ipswich station for a pre-season tour of Switzerland in 1963. They played two games, against Sparta Rotterdam and host-club FC Grenchen, winning both games 4–2 and 5–2 respectively. The dapper chap at the back in hat and sunglasses is John Cobbold.

Jackie Milburn – 'Wor Jackie' to adoring Geordie fans – takes over the manager's job at Portman Road following Alf Ramsey's departure to become England boss. Milburn's short reign at Portman Road was disastrous. He inherited an ageing squad from Ramsey and was unable to bring in enough quality replacements to stop the slide. Town were relegated from Division One in his first full season, and he resigned shortly after the start of the following season, with his health suffering. It was generally agreed that Milburn was 'far too nice to be a football manager.'

Doug Moran does not look at all comfortable balancing on a narrow bench while holding weights in this picture of an all-action training session at Portman Road in August 1963.

I do not think you will make the Olympics weightlifting squad, Ray! Crawford looks ill at ease as a muscleman at this training session in August 1963.

Town boss Jackie Milburn is presented with a gold watch at Hubbards, in Carr Street, Ipswich, in August 1963. Players looking on are Andy Nelson and Ted Phillips, along with trainer Jimmy Forsyth.

A rather grim-faced team line-up from 1963. Only Danny Hegan, second row from the back, second left, looks pleased to be there. Perhaps the rest knew what the season was to hold in store!

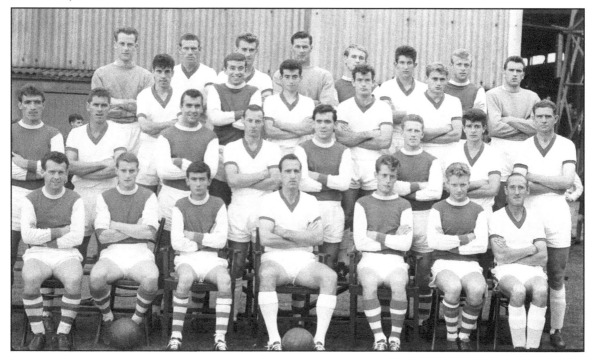

Ipswich got off to a great start to the 1963–64 season, beating Burnley 3–1 at Portman Road. The photo shows Ray Crawford scoring one of his two goals. But Town were not to win another League game until 20 December, and they were heading for the drop.

One of Ray Crawford's two goals during Town's 3–1 win over Burnley. Sadly, it was not to last.

Peter Bonetti looks like he would rather get out of the way of this blockbuster from Ted Phillips. This was October 1963, and Town were heading for relegation. This was in the middle of a dreadful winless run that lasted from August until December. Danny Hegan is Town's other attacker.

Chelsea striker Bobby Tambling watches anxiously as the ball heads towards the Town net. Tambling scored twice in Chelsea's 3–1 win at Portman Road in October 1963. The Londoners' other goal came from someone called Terry Venables. Dave Bevis is the Town 'keeper, making one of his rare appearances.

The Town 'keeper under pressure here is the barely-remembered Dave Bevis. The Southampton-born 'keeper was never on the winning side in the six League games he played for Town, as understudy for first Roy Bailey and later Ken Hancock. This was one of his unhappy games, dating from October 1963. Chelsea won 3–1 and it was going to be a very long season as Town crashed out of the top division.

The ball is in the back of the Liverpool net, and there is nothing 'keeper Tommy Lawrence or defenders Gerry Byrne (number two) or the colossus Ron Yeats (running towards the goal) can do about it. Scorer Danny Hegan is out of picture. Despite Hegan's goal, Town lost 2–1 in this clash from October 1963 to goals from Roger Hunt and Jimmy Melia.

Spurs 'keeper Bill Brown gathers the ball safely in this Portman Road game against Spurs in November 1963, while strongman Dave Mackay takes care of Ted Phillips. Spurs won 3–2, with Terry Dyson, later of Colchester, scoring twice.

Martin Peters might have been 10 years ahead of his time, according to Sir Alf Ramsey, but he is too late here to stop Doug Moran scoring for Ipswich against the Hammers at Portman Road in December 1963. 'Keeper Jim Standen is helpless. Bobby Blackwood and Gerry Baker scored Town's other goals in a 3–2 win. The celebrated World Cup-winning trio of Moore, Hurst and Peters all played for the visitors.

The day of Town's biggest humiliation – the 10–1 away defeat against Fulham on Boxing Day 1963. It was more than three decades before anything like it happened again. Remember the 9–0 defeat at Old Trafford in 1995? The two Ipswich teams involved had one unhappy thing in common – they were both heading for relegation.

Football, as they say, is indeed a funny old game. On Boxing Day 1963 Ipswich Town travelled to Craven Cottage and suffered the biggest defeat in their history, 10–1 at the hands of not-so-mighty Fulham. A mere two days later, Fulham came to Portman Road. It was the way things were done in those days. The result? A 4–2 win for Town, with goals from Baxter, Hegan, Broadfoot and Baker. Here, Fulham 'keeper Tony Macedo watches the ball safely past the post. Danny Hegan seems to be doing a rather odd little jig. George Cohen is the Fulham defender.

All smiles – but Town were going down. It was January 1964, and Jackie Milburn (far right) is presiding over a disastrous relegation season. Among the players included in this training-ground picture are Andy Nelson, Roy Bailey, Danny Hegan, and Jimmy 'Sticks' Leadbetter.

Town lost 4–1 at home to Sheffield Wednesday in January 1964. Three of Wednesday's goals were scored by their centre-forward 'Bronco' Layne. Within a few weeks, he and two of his teammates were detained at Her Majesty's pleasure for betting on their own team to lose against Ipswich just over a year earlier. This picture shows Bill Baxter trying his luck for Town.

The legend that was Stanley Matthews might have been nearing 50 when he came to Portman Road in 1964 with his Stoke City side, but he clearly still had a trick or two up his sleeve for defenders! Here, it looks as though he has skipped past Town full-back John Compton before delivering his cross. This was a fourth-round FA Cup tie which ended 1–1. Stoke won the replay 1–0.

Matthews beats Compton to the ball at Portman Road in the FA Cup.

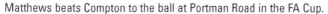

Town skipper Andy Nelson in action in the FA Cup tie against Stoke City in January 1964.

Mighty Arsenal came to Town in February 1964 and left with a 2–1 win. Gerry Baker (number nine) provided the one bright spot for home fans, scoring from close range. Ian Ure, later of Manchester United, is among the Arsenal defenders unable to prevent Baker from scoring.

Town won this game against Sheffield United 1–0 in February 1964, thanks to a penalty from Bill Baxter, but it was a temporary reprieve in a dreadful season. They lost their next two games 6–0 at Liverpool and 9–1 at Stoke.

Bill Baxter did not score many goals – a total of 22 in 459 appearances for Ipswich – but here is one of them. This photo shows him scoring the only goal of the game against Sheffield United in February 1964.

Sheffield United 'keeper Alan Hodgkinson dives to parry this Ipswich effort in a game from February 1964. Town fans enjoyed a rare victory in a season of almost unrelenting gloom. Ipswich won 1–0 thanks to Bill Baxter's goal.

Jimmy Leadbetter in rare aerial action in this game against Nottingham Forest at Portman Road in March 1964. The 4–3 win provided Town with one of only nine League wins all season. Leadbetter was one of the scorers, along with two from Bobby Blackwood and one from John Colrain.

A 4–3 win over Aston Villa in April 1964 brought some much-needed relief for Town fans as their team plummeted towards relegation. By now, crowds had dwindled and only 11,658 watched this game. In the picture, Jimmy Leadbetter is hoping for a mistake from Villa 'keeper Wilson.

Town won this game against Aston Villa 4–3 in April 1964, with goals from Joe Broadfoot (two), Gerry Baker and Bill Baxter. Sadly, it was not enough to save Ipswich from relegation that season.

The last top-flight action at Portman Road for four years. This is goal action from Town's last game of the 1963–64 season, against Blackpool. Tony Waiters is unable to prevent Gerry Baker scoring one of his hat-trick goals. It would be 1968 before Town were to taste life in the top flight again.

Town beat Blackpool 4–3 in the final game of the 1963–64 season, but it was far too late to save them from relegation. Gerry Baker scored a hat-trick in this game, and two of Blackpool's goals came from a very young player called Alan Ball. England full-back Jimmy Armfield, seen here in the centre of the photo, turned out for Blackpool that day.

1964–65: The hard man arrives

Big changes were desperately needed if what appeared to be an unstoppable slide was going to be arrested. Back in Division Two, Town failed to win any of their first eight League games, and Jackie 'too nice to be a manager' Milburn duly resigned. He was replaced by tough-guy Bill McGarry, who was under no illusions about the task that faced him. He cleared out the ageing heroes – this was the final hoorah for Roy Bailey, Larry Carberry, John Elsworthy, Jimmy Leadbetter, Andy Nelson, and Roy Stephenson – and replaced them with the likes of Frank Brogan, Mick McNeil, and Ken Hancock. After their poor start, Town picked up and eventually finished a respectable fifth in Division Two.

Gerry Baker top scored with 16 goals, with Brogan helping himself to 13, and flying winger Joe Broadfoot 12.

Division Two final position: 5th.

FA Cup: Fourth Round.

League Cup: Second Round.

It was 25 August 1964, and Town were back in the Second Division, playing against Coventry City. If these fans thought life would be easier at a lower level, they were in for a shock – Coventry won 3–1.

The old guard are still in charge – but only just. Andy Nelson and Roy Bailey snuff out a Coventry attack at Portman Road in the first home game of the 1964–65 season. Although they had been relegated back to the Second Division, Town made a disastrous start. Manager Milburn was soon gone, and stalwarts like Nelson and Bailey quickly followed. Coventry won this one 3–1.

If Town fans thought life would be easier following relegation in 1964, they were in for a nasty surprise. Ipswich did not win any of the first eight games of the 1964–65 season, and one of the heavy defeats was this 5–1 home thrashing by Preston. The unmistakable figure of Jimmy Leadbetter is in the foreground of this picture, in what was his last season following a distinguished career at Portman Road. Joe Broadfoot scored Town's only goal on a miserable afternoon. A storming second half of the season eventually saw Town finish fifth

The sun was shining – but that was the end of the good news. It was August 1964, and newly-relegated Town were finding life in the Second Division just as tough as they had in the top flight the previous season. The Blues lost this game 5–1 to a Preston team which was destined to finish in mid-table. Joe Broadfoot scored Town's only goal. Ipswich did not record a win until their ninth League game, sparking fears that they would fall straight through into the Third Division. The doom-merchants were proved wrong, however, as a revival in fortunes saw them eventually finish in a respectable fifth place.

The 1964–65 team. By now, only Bill Baxter remained from the side which took Division One by storm only three years earlier.

When Ipswich lost the local derby at Norwich 2–1 in September 1964, it proved to be the end of Jackie Milburn's short, unsuccessful and largely unhappy spell in the manager's hot seat. Having inherited an ageing squad from Ramsey, the Geordie folk hero was unable to stave off relegation. When the 1964–65 season started off equally badly, Milburn resigned. This action from his last game shows Frank Brogan and Dennis Thrower (number six) attacking the Canaries' goal. Gerry Baker put Town ahead in this game, but second-half strikes from Gordon Bolland and Welsh international Ron Davies sealed 'Wor Jackie's' fate.

Worrying times: In September 1964, Town had crashed back into the Second Division, and they could not get a result to save their lives. This crowd scene was taken at the home game against Bolton. It was the eighth game of the season, and the previous seven had yielded just three points. Surely Ipswich, champions of all England just two seasons earlier, could not plummet straight through the Second Division? Well, this game did not steady nerves – Town lost 4–1.

This was a good win for Town in October 1964, 3–1 against Newcastle United, who were to end up as Second Division champions that season. Here is Frank Brogan scoring one of the goals, despite the efforts of Newcastle 'keeper Gordon Marshall and defender Jim Iley. Former Sunderland player Danny Hegan scored the other two, one from the penalty spot.

At last, something to shout about! Town fans celebrate in October 1964 as their heroes beat visitors Newcastle 3–1.

Action from an eight-goal thriller against Rotherham in October 1964. The game ended 4–4, with Town goals coming from John Colrain (two), Danny Hegan and Joe Broadfoot. The picture shows Rotherham 'keeper Gordon Morritt collecting a cross under no pressure whatsoever from Jimmy Leadbetter.

Danny Hegan tries his luck against Rotherham United in October 1964. Hegan was one of Town's scorers in a thrilling 4–4 draw. Although Ipswich missed out on promotion that season, regular home supporters certainly got their money's worth in terms of goals. Among the games at Portman Road were a 5–2 win over Middlesbrough, a 7–0 thrashing of Portsmouth, and a 4–0 trouncing of Manchester City. The top two in the Second Division that year were the unlikely pairing of Newcastle and Northampton Town.

Following Jackie Milburn's departure, Town recruited the no-nonsense Bill McGarry as the new manager in November 1964. Here he is, on his first day at work, meeting some of the directors.

Town thumped hapless Pompey 7–0 in November 1964 to record their biggest League win – equalled since by two identical scorelines in the 1970s. Frank Brogan helped himself to a hat-trick, Danny Hegan scored two – one of which is shown here – while Joe Broadfoot and Gerry Baker were the other scorers. It was a shame that only 12,536 were there to watch it.

Welsh wing-half Cyril Lea joined Town from Leyton Orient in November 1964. He was to serve the club in a variety of roles – including caretaker manager – over the next few years. Here he is getting to know new teammate Mick McNeil.

Town beat visitors Bury 1–0 in December 1964. Town were enjoying a good season – finishing fifth – but crowds were worryingly low. Only 9,118 hardy souls braved the cold to watch this one.

Bury 'keeper Chris Harker keeps calm as a Town attack is snuffed out in December 1964. Gerry Baker scored the only goal of the game. On the visitors' teamsheet was none other than a young Colin Bell, who later found fame with Manchester City and England.

Town beat Huddersfield 3–2 in December 1964, largely thanks to the generosity of the visitors! Huddersfield scored two own-goals, courtesy of Jimmy Nicholson and John Coddington. This picture looks suspiciously like one of the 'gifts' Town enjoyed that cold, pre-Christmas afternoon.

Eagle-eyed fans of a certain vintage might recognise the leaping Huddersfield keeper from this action shot from December 1964. It is former Manchester United goalie Ray Wood. He is best remembered as the victim of an outrageously late shoulder charge by Aston Villa forward Peter McParland in the 1957 FA Cup Final. Wood's jaw was broken in the challenge. Less than a year later, he was one of the survivors of the Munich air disaster. Town won this encounter 3–2, with two own-goals from generous Huddersfield defenders, and a rare strike from Mick McNeil.

Canaries 'keeper Kevin Keelan takes charge of the situation at Portman Road in January 1965. But the long-serving Keelan was unable to stop Town winning 3–0 with two goals from Gerry Baker and one from Joe Broadfoot.

The legendary 'Swede' (left) and a fellow mascot whipping the crowd into a frenzy (or maybe not) before the East Anglian derby at Portman Road in January 1965. 'Swede' was a pre-match fixture for many seasons, although his earthy style probably would not go down well in these more politically correct days. Town won 3–1 with two goals from Gerry Baker and one from Joe Broadfoot. Ipswich finished in sixth place in the Second Division, pipping their Norfolk neighbours on goal average.

Scottish winger Frank Brogan was an important figure for Ipswich in the mid and late 1960s, regularly featuring on the scoresheet. Here he is, wearing the number-11 shirt, in the thick of the action in a game against Plymouth Argyle at Portman Road in January 1965. Brogan scored in a 2–2 draw. The other Ipswich goal was an own-goal from Plymouth's Reeves.

Flying winger Joe Broadfoot looked badly injured in this game against Plymouth in January 1965. Trainer Jimmy Forsyth looks suitably concerned. Broadfoot cannot have been too badly hurt, though, because he turned out in the next game a week later. This game ended 2–2.

Mick McNeil gives the team bus a playful polish as the Town players set off for an FA Cup tie at Spurs in January 1965. This was a chance for Ipswich to test themselves against the best following their relegation the previous season. They failed the test: Spurs won 5–0.

In January 1965, by now Second Division Town were given the chance to taste the big time again when they were drawn away at Spurs in the fourth round of the FA Cup. The gulf in class showed, however, and the Bues were thumped 5–0, with Jimmy Greaves grabbing a hat-trick and his strike partner Alan Gilzean scoring the other two. The picture shows Maurice Norman clearing what must have been a rare Town attack.

Town finished a highly respectable fifth in the Second Division in 1964–65. One of their better results was a 5–2 victory over Middlesbrough at Portman Road in February 1965. The goals came from Frank Treacy (2), Frank Brogan, Gerry Baker and Joe Broadfoot. The photo shows drama in the Middlesbrough goalmouth.

1965–66: Old hero's return, future hero's debut

Although 1965–66 was a disappointing season overall for Ipswich, there was one really big signing towards the end of the campaign. This was the return of goalscoring hero Ray Crawford after spells at Wolves and West Bromwich Albion. If any fans were wondering if he still had the goalscoring touch, then they need not have worried. Crawford scored eight times in the last 12 games of the season. Other than that, it was a less-than-memorable campaign: Town finished a lowly 15th in Division Two. Two pieces of trivia from a truly forgettable year: Dave Harper became Town's first ever substitute when he came on for Frank Brogan at Charlton on 25 August 1965, and a fresh-faced youngster called Mick Mills made his debut.

Division Two final position: 15th.

FA Cup: Third Round.

League Cup: Fifth Round.

The 1965–66 season was a poor one for Town, with them finishing 15th in the Second Division. That was one place better than Charlton, but the South Londoners had the better of an early-season encounter at The Valley, winning 2–0. The Charlton line up featured a young Billy Bonds. Our picture shows Frank Brogan trying unsuccessfully to get on the end of a cross.

Town beat visitors Plymouth 4–1 in an early-season encounter at Portman Road in September 1965. Goals came from Danny Hegan, Cyril Lea, John Colrain, and an own-goal from Plymouth's Newman, which is pictured here.

A sunny Portman Road in September 1965. Town won this game against Plymouth Argyle 4–1. Here, Danny Hegan is shown maing a nuisance of himself to a pair of Argyle defenders. It was not a good season for Town, though – they finished 15th in the Second Division.

It is fair to say that 1965–66 marked a low point in Ipswich Town's fortunes. This game against Rotherham in December 1965 just about summed it up. It ended 0–0, and only 10,279 fans bothered to turn out.

A Danny Hegan goal secured a 1–0 victory over visitors Coventry City in January 1966. Here, centre-forward Gerry Baker is trying to find a way round Coventry defender and man-mountain George Curtis – never an easy thing to do.

Danny Hegan scored the only goal of the game when Coventry came to Portman Road in January 1966. Here he is, pictured with teammate Gerry Baker, while defender Allan Harris looks on. Harris has a more famous brother – Ron 'Chopper' Harris, who spent years terrorising centre-forwards for Chelsea.

A definite low point – losing 3–2 at home to mighty Southport in an FA Cup third-round replay in January 1966. Goals from Baker and Brogan were not enough to spare Town's blushes. This photo gives a rare glimpse of Ken Thompson (number 10) in action for Town. He played 11 games before disappearing to Exeter City.

A midweek game under floodlights as Town take on Crystal Palace at Portman Road in February 1966. John Jackson punches clear to break up a Town attack. The game ended 2–2, with Town goals coming from Frank Brogan and Bobby Kellard. Midfielder Kellard had only joined Ipswich from Palace earlier that same season. In 1982, 'keeper Jackson, by then nearly 40, played one game for Town. He became the club's oldest-ever player.

The 'Chicken Run' looks sparsely populated for this home game against Birmingham City in March 1966. Records show that a paltry 9,000 people turned up, compared with more than 22,000 for the Norwich game the previous Saturday. Perhaps Birmingham were not a big attraction! The visitors won the game 1–0. Looming over the ground is the Greyfriars development, under construction.

A tribute to two Town legends: mighty Arsenal came to Portman Road in March 1966 for the joint testimonial game for John Elsworthy and Jimmy Leadbetter, both heroes of Alf Ramsey's 1961–62 League Championship-winning side. Among the Arsenal players pictured with Elsworthy and Leadbetter are Frank McLintock – looking remarkably similar to the way he is today – George 'Geordie' Armstrong, John Radford, and, far right, Grundisburgh-born Jon Sammels.

Ray Crawford in typical goalscoring action against Orient in April 1966. Town won 3–1, with Crawford scoring twice. But it was a poor season, with Ipswich finishing 15th in Division Two.

A wholehearted challenge from Ray Crawford seems to have the Cardiff defence at sixes and sevens in April 1966. Town won the game 2–1, with goals coming from Gerry Baker and a Bill Baxter penalty.

Frank Brogan does his best to connect with a cross in this game against Cardiff in April 1966.

In 1965–66, Manchester City stormed to the Second Division Championship as the building blocks were laid for their later triumphs on a bigger stage. So, a 1–1 draw in April 1966 was a decent result for Town. Ray Crawford was the Ipswich goalscorer. Here, Eddie Spearritt fails to get the better of the Man City defence.

What appears to be the entire playing staff on the Portman Road practice pitch at the end of the 1965–66 season. Although Town finished a lowly 15th in the Second Division, the photograph offers some optimism for the future: smiling broadly from the front row are three youngsters called Mills, Viljoen and Jefferson. In the second row is the returning Crawford. All four would play big parts in McGarry's revival.

1966–67: Draw specialists

This was a vast improvement, with Ipswich finishing fifth in Division Two, nine points behind champions Coventry City. Crawford showed he had lost none of his old goalscoring prowess, finding the net 21 times in the League. Baker and Brogan also made double figures. The most frustrating aspect of the season was Town's inability to turn draws into wins. They drew no fewer than 16 of their games in the League, including a spell between Boxing Day and 18 March when they drew eight of their nine games, losing the other one. A very significant debut came when young South African midfielder Colin Viljoen lined up for the first time in a blue shirt against Portsmouth on 25 March and celebrated with a hat-trick. Billy Houghton and Charlie Woods both arrived at Portman Road.

Division Two final position: 5th.

FA Cup: Fifth Round.

League Cup: Third Round.

It does not look like the warmest of summer days as Ipswich Town players report back for the dreaded first day of pre-season training in July 1966. Among those in the front row are the recently returned Ray Crawford and club captain Bill Baxter.

Young fans stoking up the atmosphere before local rivals Ipswich Town and Colchester United do battle in a pre-season friendly in August 1966. These young enthusiasts had a challenge on their hands – only 4,000 people turned up to watch Town win 3–1.

Ray Crawford in action in a pre-season friendly against Colchester United in 1966. Spot the crowd!

Town players with the Paisley Cup, pre-season 1966. Note baby-faced Mick Mills peering out over the trophy – he looks barely out of nappies!

This is the 1966–67 season, and things are looking up. Crawford has returned, with his goalscoring prowess undiminished, and youngsters like Danny Hegan, pictured in the background, are making an impression. Town would go up the following season. This game, against Bristol City, ended 1–1, with Gerry Baker on the scoresheet.

Ray Crawford's return to his home-town club Portsmouth in October 1966 was not a happy affair. The home team won 4–2, with Gerry Baker getting both of Town's goals. Here, Crawford is challenging Pompey 'keeper John Milkins.

Gerry Baker has just scored one of Town's two goals at Portsmouth in October 1966 – the striker can be seen running away to celebrate. Baker's pair were not enough, though, as Portsmouth went on to win 4–2. It was not a happy return to Fratton Park for either Ray Crawford or Mick Mills.

Hull 'keeper Ian Mckechnie looks around helplessly as Frank Brogan celebrates one of his two goals in Town's thrilling 5–4 victory over Hull City in October 1966. Charlie Woods is the other celebrating Ipswich player.

How is this for luxury! The Town squad leaving Ipswich Airport in October 1967 for the match against Plymouth Argyle. A Ray Crawford goal secured a point. A very youthful Mick Mills was the unlucky 13th man who missed out on any action at Home Park.

One of the most exciting games of the 1966–1967 season was this nine-goal thriller against Hull City. Town eventually won 5–4, with a Ray Crawford hat-trick and two from Frank Brogan. Both are heavily involved in the goalmouth action here. Hull's line-up included goalkeeper Ian Mckechnie and the twin strikers Ken Wagstaff and Chris Chilton. Wagstaff scored two of Hull's goals that day. The Hull line up would become very familiar to Suffolk football fans, when the Tigers appeared regularly on Anglia TV's *Match of the Week* programme on Sunday afternoons. No one ever really explained how Hull came to be classed as East Anglia!

There were real fireworks on 5 November 1966 as Town hit hapless Northampton for six at Portman Road. Scottish winger Frank Brogan helped himself to a hat-trick. One of his goals is pictured here. Northampton went down at the end of the season.

Mick McNeil puts in a sold challenge in a game against Rotherham United in November 1966, with fellow defender Bill Baxter ready to lend a helping hand. Town won the game 3–0, with Billy Houghton, Gerry Baker and Ray Crawford on target.

Ray Crawford seems to be playing a game of leapfrog in this game against Rotherham United in November 1966.

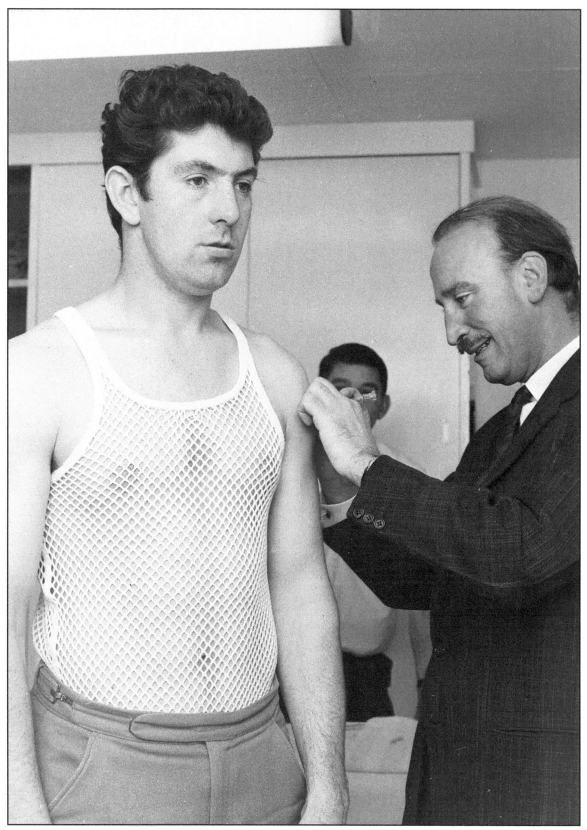

Nice vest, Ken! 'Keeper Hancock is being a brave boy as he is given his flu jab in December 1966.

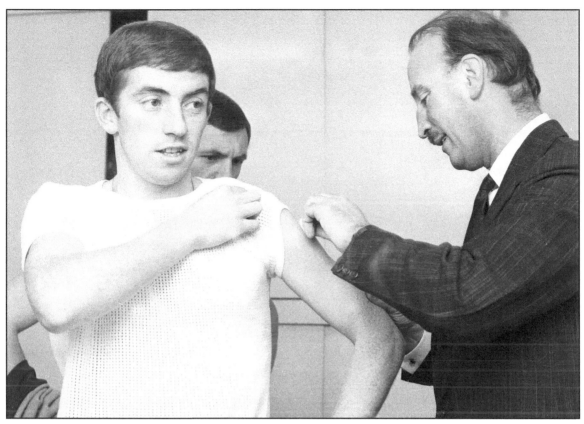

Danny Hegan puts on a brave face as he is given his flu jab just before Christmas 1966. Charlie Woods, next in line, does not look quite so sure.

Bury 'keeper Ramsbottom collects the ball safely in this game at Portman Road from December 1966. He could do nothing to stop Gerry Baker and Ray Crawford scoring Town's goals in a 2–0 win, though.

In December 1966, visitors Bury were beaten 2–0, thanks to goals from strike partners Gerry Baker and Ray Crawford. Bury finished rock bottom that year. Here is Crawford making a nuisance of himself with Charlie Woods looking on.

It must be a goal! But, somehow, it was not. Town were held 0–0 by visitors Cardiff in December 1966. John Toshack featured for the visitors.

Another view of the goalmouth action against Cardiff City in December 1966.

A funny moment from a dull game. A Bristol City defender is either thinking of taking up a new career in dance, or is determined to do himself a nasty injury. This is action from Town's home game against the West Country side in January 1967. It ended 0–0.

Ray Crawford terrorising the Shrewsbury defence in this FA Cup game from January 1967. Town won 4–1. The crowd in the 'Chicken Run' looks a bit sparse. The attendance was 14,906.

The crowd at Portman Road for the FA Cup third-round tie against Shrewsbury Town in January 1967. These fans went home happy: Ipswich won 4–1, with goals from Frank Brogan, Ray Crawford, Dave Harper and Danny Hegan.

The Ipswich Town forward line training in February 1967. They are Joe Broadfoot, Danny Hegan, Ray Crawford, Gerry Baker and Frank Brogan.

Blackburn 'keeper Barton punches clear under pressure from Ray Crawford in this Second Division clash from February 1967. Crawford was on target in a 1–1 draw.

Ray Crawford and Joe Broadfoot contest a cross against Blackburn at Portman Road in February 1967. Crawford scored in a 1–1 draw. The changing Ipswich skyline looms above the 'Chicken Run'. This tiny stand was replaced by the Cobbold Stand in 1971 and moved to the speedway stadium at Foxhall. The structure came a real cropper in the 'hurricane' of October 1987.

Joe Broadfoot has taken a tumble, but the ref is waving play on. This is Ipswich versus Blackburn, from February 1967. It ended 1–1, with Ray Crawford scoring Town's goal.

Crawford was back in Town colours, and suddenly things were looking up again. Here he is scoring to secure a 1–1 draw against Blackburn in February 1967. Town went on to finish fifth in the Second Division, before winning the title the following season. Blackburn fielded three England internationals: Keith Newton, Ronnie Clayton, and John Connelly.

A sorry sight for Town fans – Danny Hegan being stretchered off at Blackburn in February 1967. Mick McNeil is offering Hegan a few encouraging words, but coach Sammy Chung appears less than concerned. Town drew the game 1–1, with Ray Crawford scoring the goal.

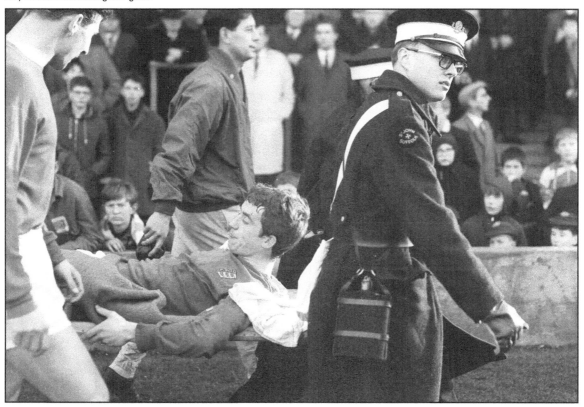

Gerry Baker seems to have the beating of Carlisle 'keeper Ross in this FA Cup fourth-round tie at Portman Road in February 1967. Baker did not feature on the scoresheet, however, and Town's goals in a 2–0 win came from Ray Crawford and Frank Brogan. Among those featuring for Carlisle were the footballer-cricketer Chris Balderstone and diminutive midfielder Wille Carlin, who was later to become an integral part of Brian Clough's successful Derby County side. Carlin did not enjoy a happy afternoon at Portman Road, however, as his side lost, and he was sent off in the last minute.

A real mix of generations among the Ipswich Town fans at this FA Cup tie against Carlisle United in February 1967. The one thing they all have in common – young and old alike – is that they are all smartly turned out. It is unlikely that as many shirts and ties would be seen at Portman Road these days! Town won the game 2–0 to set up a fifth-round game at Manchester City.

A big day – Town fans set off for Maine Road for the FA Cup fifth-round game against Manchester City in March 1967. The Suffolk side held their First Division opponents 1–1, with a goal from Ray Crawford, before crashing 3–0 in the replay at Portman Road.

Cyril Lea leads out the team for the fifth-round FA Cup tie at Manchester City in March 1967.

Ray Crawford challenges Manchester City 'keeper Alan Ogley for a cross in the FA Cup fifth-round tie at Maine Road in March 1967. The Manchester City line up already contained several of the stars who Joe Mercer and Malcolm Allison managed to further glories.

Muddy, battered, but unbowed. Town's players celebrate a notable result after holding Manchester City to a 1–1 draw in the fifth round of the FA Cup at Maine Road in 1967.

Colin Viljoen proved the scourge of Pompey when they came to Portman Road in March 1967, helping himself to a hat-trick on his debut. Here he is terrorising the defence.

Not a bad start! Here is the South African midfielder scoring one of his hat-trick against Portsmouth in a 4–2 win at Portman Road in March 1967. Ray Crawford, also pictured, scored the other one.

Ray Crawford shoots – and, for once, does not score. This game against Preston, at Portman Road at the end of the 1966–67 season, finished goalless.

1967–68: Division Two champions again

Bill McGarry steered Ipswich to the top of Division Two and back to the big time. Mind you, it was a close-run thing before Town eventually clinched the Second Division Championship: they finished a single point ahead of Queen's Park Rangers, who in turn edged out Blackpool on goal average. The key was a long, 15-match unbeaten run at the end of the season. Town's last League defeat was at Carlisle on 10 February. McGarry made two crucial signings during the run-in, midfield dynamo Peter Morris from Mansfield and striker John O'Rourke from Middlesbrough. O'Rourke scored 12 goals in the 15 games he played. Frank Brogan top scored with 17 in the League, pipping Ray Crawford by one.

Division Two final position: 1st.

FA Cup: Third Round.

League Cup: Third Round.

Glory beckons: The Ipswich squad, plus coaching staff and directors, pictured at the beginning of the 1967–68 season. Nine months later, Town would be back in the First Division.

Action from a pre-season friendly from August 1967 against Belgian side La Gantoise. They are now known as K.A.A Ghent. Whatever they were called in 1967, they were not very good. Town won 7–0. The scorers are not recorded, but it is pretty certain that Ray Crawford, in the action here, was on the scoresheet.

Ron Wigg has just scored one of his two goals against Carlisle in September 1967. Town won the game 3–1, with Eddie Spearritt, who is on the left of this picture, getting the other one.

Two of Town's all-time greats. Bill Baxter and Ray Crawford both played key roles in Alf Ramsey's Division One-winning team in 1962 and were reunited when Bill McGarry brought back the good times in 1968, when Town returned to the top flight. Crawford is the club's all-time leading goalscorer, while Baxter was a stalwart for more than a decade and is generally regarded as being unlucky not to have won senior caps for Scotland.

Ray Crawford in typical action against Carlisle on a sunny afternoon at Portman Road in September 1967. Town won 3–1 and, unusually, Crawford was not on the scoresheet.

A crucial moment in Bill McGarry's rebuilding exercise – Colin Viljoen signing on the dotted line in 1967, watched over by a clearly delighted McGarry. South African Viljoen, nicknamed 'Ace', was a key player for Town over the next decade, helping them regain First Division status, and also being central to Robson's first successful team. He went on to win two England caps. But his Town career ended in controversy when he was picked for the final League game before the 1978 FA Cup Final at the expense of Roger Osborne. His teammates were not impressed, and the result was a 6–1 thumping at Aston Villa, during which Viljoen saw precious little of the ball. Osborne was reinstated for the Wembley Final and the rest, as they say, is history.

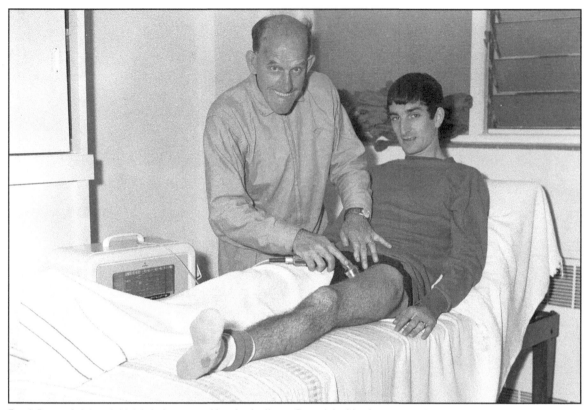

Frank Brogan's injured thigh is being treated by physio Jimmy Forsyth in this picture from September 1967. It is probably fair to say that medical treatment of players has come quite a long way since then.

A rare sight of striker Bobby Hunt in action against Aston Villa in November 1967. Hunt was bought from Millwall to pep up the Town attack but only managed four goals in four seasons. Bill McGarry turned to John O'Rourke, with rather more successful results. Town won this game 2–1, with goals from Eddie Spearritt and Frank Brogan.

For once, Ray is off target. This Crawford header against Aston Villa in November 1967 failed to register, but Crawford did score 16 goals as Town returned to the First Division. Frank Brogan, also pictured, was top scorer, with 17, and new signing John O'Rourke weighed in with 12 towards the end of a memorable season. The Town player in the middle of the picture is Bobby Hunt, who failed to impress after signing from Millwall.

Ray Crawford seems to be having difficulty keeping his feet in slippery conditions in this game against his old team, Portsmouth, in December 1967. The snowy conditions brought a rare home defeat for Town in this promotion-winning season. Colin Viljoen is the other Ipswich player pictured.

Two goals from Frank Brogan gave Ipswich victory in this Boxing Day clash with Millwall at Portman Road in 1967. Eddie Spearritt is the Town player putting in the challenge here, with Brogan lurking in the background.

After signing from Millwall, striker Bobby Hunt scored just one goal for Ipswich Town in the 1967–68 season – against Millwall. Here he is, fighting a former teammate for the ball on his return to the Den. The game ended 1–1.

Little Danny Hegan in aerial combat in the Town versus Millwall game at the Den, on 30 December 1967. Those were the days when teams played each other twice in the space of a few days over Christmas. In that season, Town beat Millwall 2–1 at Portman Road on Boxing Day and grabbed a point in a 1–1 away draw four days later.

Town players being fitted with very smart suits at Coes in Ipswich in December 1967. The 'look' even included a monogram on the breast pocket! The ski boots which appear in the bottom left-hand corner of the photo were not part of the package!

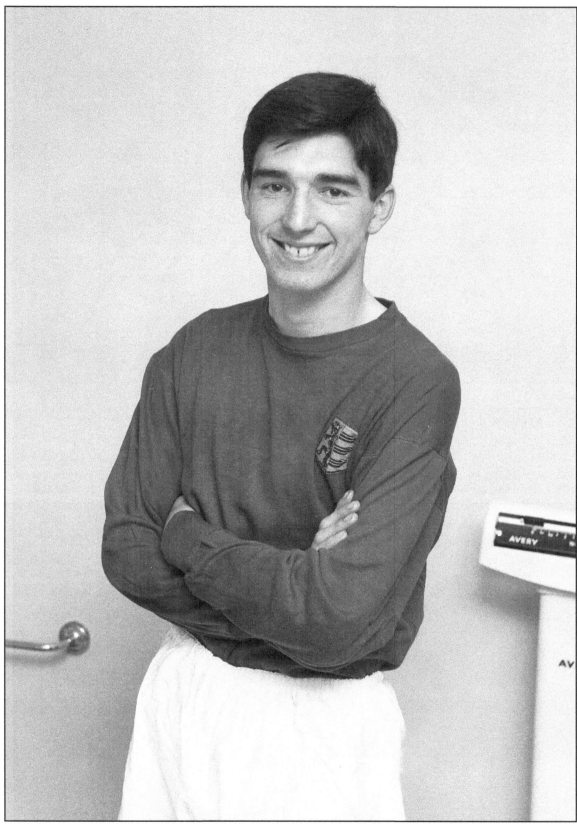

A very youthful Mick Lambert in December 1967. The boy from Cambridgeshire made his Town debut in March 1969 and went on to make more than 250 appearances in a long career with the club. He famously appeared as substitute in the 1978 FA Cup Final, replacing the exhausted goal hero Roger Osborne.

Town's players and coaching staff are in high spirits at the beginning of a golf day at Bury St Edmunds Golf Club, shortly before Christmas 1967. No one appears to have told them that they would need more than one club each!

What would Cristiano Ronaldo have made of this? In the days before footballers earned ridiculous amounts of money, they were grateful for hand-outs from generous local businesses. Here, Town's first-team squad are presented with Christmas turkeys in 1967. The line-up from left is: Mick McNeil, Frank Brogan, Ray Crawford, who is proudly holding the unfortunate turkey, unknown, Bobby Hunt (who appears transfixed by the bird's feet!), Bill Baxter, Billy Houghton, Tommy Carroll, Danny Hegan and Eddie Spearritt. On their knees, for some unknown reason, are Ken Hancock and Cyril Lea.

Town players enjoying a party at the Birchwood Hotel, Ardleigh, in February 1968. Joe Broadfoot has grabbed the microphone, while the young lady on the left, beauty queen Nanette Slack, is about to put her favourite 'discs' on the record player.

Town's FA Cup 'run' in 1968 lasted precisely one game – leaving them to concentrate on gaining promotion. Ipswich came a cropper at Stamford Bridge, when Chelsea beat them 3–0 in the third round. Here, home 'keeper Peter Bonetti punches clear under pressure from Mick Mills and Ray Crawford. Legendary hard man Ron 'Chopper' Harris is also lending his support.

Town's visit to the Baseball Ground in March 1968 saw them come away with a hard-fought 3–2 victory, with two goals from Frank Brogan and one from John O'Rourke. This was Brian Clough's first full season in charge at Derby, and he did not work his magic instantly. Derby finished 18th in the Second Division in this season. But a mere four years later, Clough had them sitting pretty as League Champions. The picture shows Colin Viljoen taking on the Derby defence, apparently single-handed.

Ray Crawford contests a high ball in this game against Charlton Athletic at The Valley in March 1968. Frank Brogan scored the only goal of the game.

Colin Viljoen looks certain to score in this game against Charlton Athletic in March 1968. But, somehow, the South African midfielder failed to find the net. Town did win the game, however, with Frank Brogan scoring the only goal.

Hard-man defender Derek Jefferson runs out to face Bolton Wanderers at Burnden Park in March 1968. Town, heading for promotion, won the game 2–1, with John O'Rourke scoring twice. It was part of a 15-game unbeaten run which would see Ipswich clinch the Second Division title.

Frank Brogan whips in a cross against Bolton (away) in March 1968. Town's victory was part of an unstoppable winning surge which took them to the Second Division Championship.

Danny Hegan and Ken Hancock being made to look beautiful at Payne's Hairdressers in Ipswich in April 1968. The young chap wielding the scissors on the right is local footballing (and haircutting) legend Mick Banthorpe. The other scissor-wielding chap is 'Gino'.

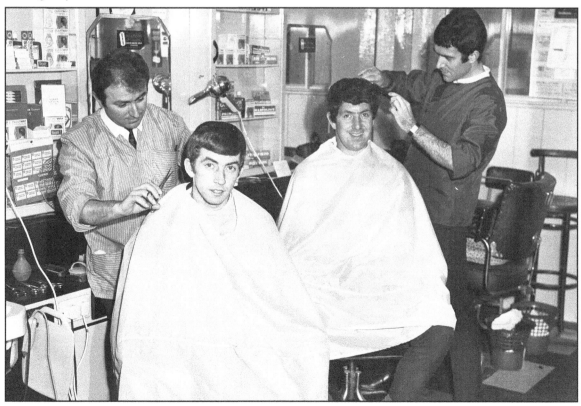

New signing Peter Morris pictured in an Ipswich Town shirt for the first time in March 1968. 'Diesel', as he was nicknamed, played a big part in Town's promotion that season and also featured prominently in Robson's first successful sides in the early 1970s.

It was April 1968, and the run-in towards the Second Division Championship for Town. Ray Crawford (number nine) has just scored yet another vital goal which helped to secure a 2–2 draw at Villa Park. John O'Rourke looks pretty pleased too.

John O'Rourke fails to beat Villa 'keeper Withers in this Second Division clash from April 1968. The game finished 2–2 as Town edged closer towards promotion.

These huge queues show the level of interest generated by Town's home game against promotion rivals Queen's Park Rangers in April 1968. The game ended 2–2.

Ray Crawford's return to Portman Road played a crucial part in restoring the good times. Crawford, and his goalscoring partner Ted Phillips, had scored hundreds of goals as Ipswich rampaged through the divisions in the late 1950s and early 1960s under the inspirational leadership of Alf Ramsey. Crawford came back to Town in 1966, and two years later his goals helped the team get back to the top flight. Here he is in aerial battle in the 2–2 draw against promotion rivals Queen's Park Rangers in April 1968.

Ray Crawford and John O'Rourke terrorising the Queen's Park Rangers defence in the vital top-of-the-table Second Division clash at Portman Road in April 1968. Crawford and O'Rourke were both on target in a 2–2 draw. Two weeks later, Town had clinched promotion.

John O'Rourke celebrates a vital goal against Second Division promotion rivals Queen's Park Rangers' in April 1968. New signing O'Rourke's goals proved crucial in propelling Town to the title. Could Queen's Park Rangers's disconsolate number 10 be the one and only Rodney Marsh? If so, what on earth was he doing so far back?

John O'Rourke tries his luck in the game that clinched Town's return to the top flight. A 1–1 draw against Blackburn Rovers was enough to seal the Second Division title.

The ball is in the back of Blackburn's net, and the celebrations are about to start. Although John O'Rourke is the happy Town player pictured, this is Ray Crawford's goal. It secured a 1–1 draw for Town on the final day of the 1967–68 season, which was enough to clinch the Second Division title, one point ahead of Queen's Park Rangers, who went up after finishing second, and Blackpool, who unluckily missed out on promotion on goal average. 27,952 happy Ipswich fans watched this match.

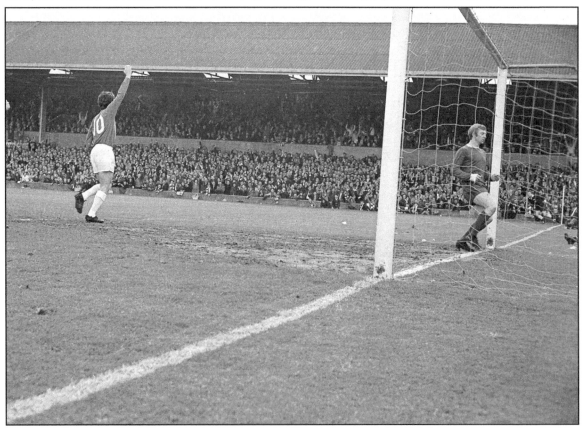

Ray Crawford in typically combative style against Blackburn Rovers in the final game of the 1967–68 promotion season. Crawford scored the crucial goal to secure a 1–1 draw and clinch a return to Division One.

Ray Crawford looks like he has lost out in this aerial duel against Blackburn – the final game of the triumphant 1967–68 season. Later that afternoon, Town were celebrating their return to the top flight.

Ray Crawford is well and truly the centre of attention as Town celebrate winning the Division Two title in May 1968.

John O'Rourke is hoisted aloft as the celebrations begin. Town have just secured a return to the top flight after four years in Division Two. O'Rourke's 12 goals late in the 1967–68 season were crucial.

It was 11 May 1968, and the Town players sprint off the pitch to avoid being mobbed by fans after winning the Second Division title. Derek Jefferson looks chuffed, but Bill Baxter keeps his cool.

Back in the big time! Town had just drawn 1–1 against Blackburn Rovers on 11 May 1968 to secure the Second Division Championship. Among those being mobbed by the celebrating crowd is the goalscorer that day, Ray Crawford.

The bubbly is flowing as Town celebrate winning the Second Division Championship in 1968. From the left: Bill Baxter, Ken Hancock, Billy Houghton, John O'Rourke, trainer Sammy Chung, manager Bill McGarry, Danny Hegan, Tommy Carroll, Ray Crawford and Frank Brogan.

For some reason, Danny Hegan's number-seven shirt is the centre of attention as Hegan, John O'Rourke and Ken Hancock get stuck into the celebrations after Town clinch the Second Division title in May 1968. From the look of Hancock's jacket, the knees-up is in full swing!

Fans celebrate in May 1968 as Ipswich Town return to the top flight.

Town chairman 'Mr John' Cobbold looks unusually hesitant about his tipple during the dressing room celebrations after Town clinched the Second Division Championship in May 1968. Players Derek Jefferson, John O'Rourke, Danny Hegan, Bill Houghton, and Ken Hancock look more eager to get stuck in.

Good clean fun. Peter Morris, Ray Crawford and Bill Baxter are in good spirits after clinching their return to Division One in May 1968. Danny Hegan seems rather preoccupied by his drink.

Cheers! Town's victorious Second Division champions letting their hair down at a celebration at the Copdock Hotel in May 1968.

We are the champions! Ipswich players at the legendary First Floor Club in Ipswich after clinching a return to the First Division in May 1968. The man with the microphone is club owner Ken Bean.

Here is your reward for winning the Second Division Championship, lads – a nice big juicy steak! What would today's highly-paid Premier League superstars have made of this? The lucky recipients are, from the left: Peter Morris, Danny Hegan, and Ken Hancock, pictured at a butcher's shop on the Chantry Estate in Ipswich in May 1968.

Celebrations as the Town players parade the Second Division Championship trophy through Ipswich town centre in May 1968. Bill McGarry, the man who masterminded the promotion-winning campaign, is staying out of the spotlight – you can just see him in the bottom left of the picture.

The 1967–68 squad that won promotion back to Division One. Back row, from the left: Bobby Hunt, Tommy Carroll, Derek Jefferson, Ken Hancock, Bill Baxter, Mick McNeil, Billy Houghton, Eddie Spearritt. Seated, middle, from the left: John O'Rourke, Ray Crawford, Colin Viljoen, Frank Brogan. Seated, front, from the left: Mick Mills, Danny Hegan, Peter Morris, Chris Barnard.

1968–69: Back in the big time

Ipswich consolidated in the First Division, finishing a respectable 12th, while Queen's Park Rangers, promoted with Town, ended up rock bottom. Crawford and O'Rourke finished joint-top scorers, with 16 League goals each, but Crawford departed for Charlton in February. Mick Mills established himself in the side, and 'keeper David Best arrived from Oldham Athletic. But the big shock came midway through the season, when manager Bill McGarry upped sticks and left for Wolves, claiming they were a bigger club with more chance of playing European football. The next decade and a bit would prove him wrong. After being turned down by a number of experienced managers, Town chairman 'Mr John' Cobbold took a chance by appointing rookie Bobby Robson, who had been sacked by Fulham.

Division One final position: 12th.

FA Cup: Third Round.

League Cup: Second Round.

Pre-season training with a difference. There is a slight generation gap in this bowls match involving Town players in the summer of 1968. Bill McGarry is the man taking the lead, watched by some of his players (they are the younger ones) and expert bowlers.

And this is how to tackle…Trainer Sammy Chung takes charge as first-teamer John O'Rourke shows off his skills to a group of apprentices on a hot pre-season day in July 1968. Among those trying hard to look impressed are Geoff Hammond, Bobby Bell, John Miller, Laurie Sivell, and Steve Buttle.

Town played Arbroath in a pre-season friendly in August 1968, winning 4–3, with Frank Brogan scoring a hat-trick. This picture shows Ray Crawford in action.

Frank Brogan leading the Arbroath defence a merry dance in a pre-season friendly in August 1968.

As they geared up for their return to the top flight, Town's players boarded their coach for a pre-season tour. From left to right, the players are: Peter Morris, Mick Mills, Derek 'Chopper' Jefferson (looking harmless in his horn-rimmed glasses), Mick McNeil, Bill Baxter, Ray Crawford, Ken Hancock, Tommy Carroll, Chris Barnard and Colin Viljoen. Standing on the bus are Billy Houghton and Eddie Spearritt. The players are wearing the smart suits provided by Coes.

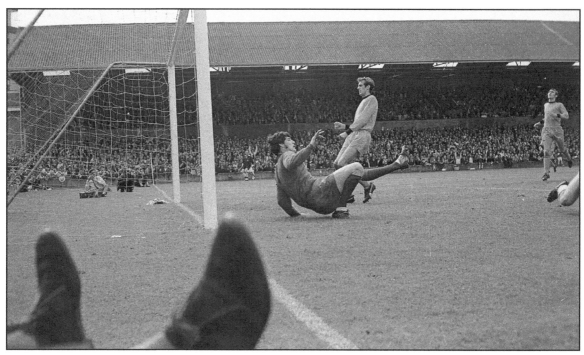

A winning start. It was Town's first game back in Division One after four years in the wilderness. John O'Rourke (not in picture) had just put the ball past Wolves 'keeper Phil Parkes for the winner. This was August 1968.

Town are back in the big time – and they are off to a flyer. John O'Rourke has just scored the winner in the opening game of the 1968–69 season against Wolves at Portman Road. The Wolves defenders look suitably upset, and Colin Viljoen is about to congratulate O'Rourke – once he has sorted out his nasal issues.

Town are back in the First Division after a four-year wait, and these supporters look very pleased about it! This is the scene in August 1968, when Ipswich welcomed Wolves to Portman Road for the first game of the season. The fans are celebrating John O'Rourke's winner.

They did not come any bigger and meaner than Leeds United back in 1968. Town lost 3–2 at home in an early-season encounter. This picture shows Gary Sprake being bailed out by a headless teammate (Paul Reaney, perhaps?) clearing off the line. Colin Viljoen, John O'Rourke, Terry Cooper and Jack Charlton are close by.

Frank Brogan tries his luck against Leeds in August 1968. The hard men from Leeds left Suffolk with a 3–2 win, despite goals from John O'Rourke and Ray Crawford, who is also pictured here. The Leeds defenders are Jack Charlton and Paul Reaney. Of course, Crawford had a really nasty surprise waiting for Leeds a couple of years later, after he had joined Colchester.

Leeds United were just about the toughest team around in the late 1960s – in more ways than one! Town discovered that to their cost when the Yorkshire side came to Portman Road in August 1968 and won 3–2, despite being weakened by injuries. Here Leeds 'keeper Gary Sprake makes a flying save with O'Rourke in the thick of the action. The Leeds defenders are Terry Cooper and Norman 'Bites Yer Legs' Hunter.

Action from one of Town's early games back in the First Division in August 1968. Ray Crawford challenges, but the ball is safely in hands of Arsenal 'keeper Bob Wilson. Arsenal won 2–1, with goals from John Radford and David Jenkins.

A rare sight of reserve striker Bobby Hunt turning out for the first team. This is Town versus Arsenal at Portman Road in August 1968.

Bobby Hunt and John O'Rourke are thwarted by this acrobatic clearance in the 2–1 home defeat against Arsenal in August 1968. The other Gunners defender is Bob McNab.

The 1968–69 season saw Town back among football's aristocracy, including mighty Arsenal, who came to Portman Road in August. The Gunners line up that day was: Bob Wilson, Peter Storey, Bob McNab, Frank McLintock, Terry Neill, Peter Simpson, John Radford, Jon Sammels, Bobby Gould, David Court and David Jenkins. With a few exceptions, this was the line up which memorably won the League and Cup double just two years later. The picture shows Danny Hegan being thwarted by Peter Simpson.

In August 1968 Town were back in the big time and on their way to beating visitors Queen's Park Rangers 3–0. Here we see Danny Hegan about to head in Town's second. Grounded 'keeper Mike Kelly is helpless. Ray Crawford is the other Town player.

England 'keeper Gordon Banks seems to be juggling the ball in this game from September 1968. The Town player in the foreground is Eddie Spearritt, while strike partners John O'Rourke and Ray Crawford are also pictured. Crawford scored twice in Town's 3–1 win against perennial strugglers Stoke. The other goal came from a Frank Brogan penalty.

Spot the World Cup legend. Yes, it is Gordon Banks leaving the pitch at Portman Road after conceding three goals. Ipswich won this game 3–1 in September 1968, although you would never know it from the glum faces of Tommy Carroll, Bill Baxter and Colin Viljoen. At least Ken Hancock manages to look a bit more cheerful.

Close, but not close enough. This effort fizzes wide of Liverpool 'keeper Tommy Lawrence's goal in this first Division game at Portman Road in September 1968. John O'Rourke has his arms raised more in hope than expectation, while Ian St John is the other Liverpool player in the picture.

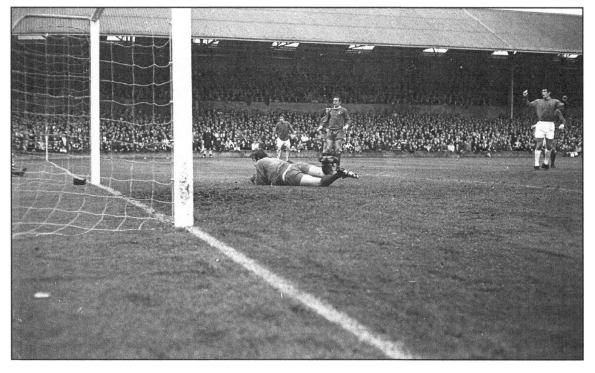

Mighty Liverpool handed Town a footballing lesson when they won 2–0 at Portman Road in September 1968, with goals from Ian St John and Bobby Graham. World Cup winner Roger Hunt was among the Liverpool stars on show that day. In this picture, Town striker John O'Rourke challenges Liverpool 'keeper Tommy Lawrence.

Scottish striker Alan Gilzean scored the only goal of the game when Spurs came to Portman Road in October 1968. Here, Gilzean is helping out at the other end of the pitch, heading clear from John O'Rourke. Alan Mullery is close at hand, and Jimmy Greaves is in the background. Frank Brogan is the Town player in close attendance.

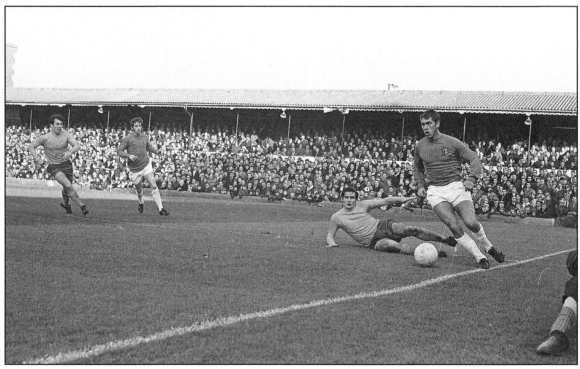

Ray Crawford has escaped the attentions of Everton defender John Hurst and is bearing down on goal in the game against the Merseysiders in November 1968. Danny Hegan and Howard Kendall are the other players pictured. Crawford and Peter Morris scored Town's goals in a 2–2 draw. Everton's goals both came from someone called Joe Royle – whatever happened to him?

Colin Viljoen climbs high against Everton and England centre-half Brian Labone in this photo from November 1968. Ray Crawford is close by, and in the background is a very youthful Howard Kendall – complete with hair!

Town 'keeper David Best collects this corner under pressure from Everton's John Hurst in this picture from November 1968. Bill Baxter, Derek Jefferson and Mick Mills are other Town defenders in close attendance, while Billy Houghton guards the line. There is no sign of a certain Joe Royle, who scored both of Everton's goals in an exciting 2–2 draw.

Everton 'keeper Gordon West and Ipswich stirker John O'Rourke challenge for the ball in the 2–2 draw at Portman Road on 9 November 1968.

John O'Rourke and Bill Baxter in an aerial duel with West Ham's John Cushley at Portman Road in November 1968. World Cup winner Martin Peters is the other player involved. Town were down and apparently out at half-time, with Geoff Hurst putting the Hammers two up. But goals from Peter Morris and Colin Viljoen rescued a point for Town. A certain Bobby Moore was at the heart of the West Ham defence.

West Ham 'keeper Bobby Ferguson punches clear in this game at Portman Road in November 1968. John O'Rourke is airborne, while Bobby Moore next to him has realised it is simply not worth the effort. The game finished 2–2, in front of a crowd of nearly 29,000.

Colin Viljoen shows off his skills against West Ham in November 1968. The game finished 2–2, and Viljoen scored one of Town's goals. The South African was to finish as leading scorer in the next two seasons, with the grand totals of six and 10 goals. To say Ipswich were struggling in front of goal is something of an understatement.

Spot the legend: England's World Cup-winning captain Bobby Moore is among the players awaiting the outcome of this aerial clash at Portman Road in November 1968.

West Brom 'keeper John Osborne makes a safe catch despite the efforts of John O'Rourke in this game from December 1968. O'Rourke had the last laugh, though, scoring twice in a 4–1 win.

One of Town's most convincing performances of the 1968–69 season was this 4–1 thrashing of West Brom at Portman Road in December 1968. John O'Rourke grabbed two goals, with the others coming from Frank Brogan and Colin Viljoen. Here is Viljoen getting his shot in, despite the efforts of West Brom defender John Talbut. Included in the visitors' line up that day was Hawthorns legend Jeff Astle, and Ian Collard, who was to join Town a few months later. In goal for West Brom was John Osborne, who was still between the sticks for the West Midlanders six years later when they came to Portman Road and were beaten 7–0, with Trevor Whymark scoring four. How Osborne must have looked forward to his visits to Suffolk!

Ray Crawford tries in vain to get his toe to the ball in this game against Nottingham Forest at Portman Road shortly before Christmas 1968. The Forest 'keeper is Peter Grummitt. Forest won the game 3–2, despite goals from Hegan and Morris.

The famed Portman Road pitch looks far from its best in this shot from the Boxing Day game against Chelsea in 1968. Ray Crawford is on the ball, but the game's crucial figure is lurking behing him: David Webb, the Chelsea centre-half, who scored a hat-trick that day.

Those were the days! Blizzard conditions at Portman Road for the game against Chelsea on Boxing Day 1968. The match did not do much to warm Town fans up – the Londoners won 3–1, with a hat-trick from David Webb, who was a defender. This was during Cyril Lea's spell as caretaker manager, following Bill McGarry's resignation and pending the arrival of a certain Bobby Robson.

Ray Crawford soaring high during Town's 2–0 win over Burnley on a grim-looking day in January 1969. It was Robson's first home game – and his first win. Crawford scored the first Ipswich goal, and the second came from Mick Mills. It was his first goal for the senior side – and not all that many were to follow over the next 13 years!

A dank January day in 1969, and a new manager arrives. Bobby Robson has just stepped off the train at Ipswich station to be met by chairman John Cobbold. It was the start of something big!

A momentous day in the history of Ipswich Town Football Club. It was January 1969 and Bobby Robson's first day as manager. It is easy to forget now, but he came with a less-than-distinguished managerial track record, and was far from being first choice for Town, who would have preferred a rather more established name like Frank O'Farrell or Billy Bingham. Still, it all turned out quite well in the end.

A new era dawns on a misty day in January 1969, and Town are on their way to a 2–0 win over Burnley at Portman Road, with goals from Crawford and Mills. This was to be one of Crawford's last games for Ipswich, as he moved to Charlton a few weeks later. The picture shows John O'Rourke challenging for the ball, with Colin Viljoen awaiting developments. The new era? This was Robson's first home game.

John O'Rourke and Danny Hegan are in the thick of the action in this game against Manchester United in February 1969. Tony Dunne's own-goal settled matters in favour of Town. United were on the slide.

The ball is trickling into the Manchester United net, despite the best efforts of Alex Stepney and Nobby Stiles. Chris Barnard is looking pleased with life. This was the own-goal from Tony Dunne which gave Town a 1–0 victory over United at Portman Road in February 1969. On paper this was a notable scalp, as United were still European Cup holders, but, in reality, decline had set in, and the Red Devils only managed to finish 11th in Division One that season, one point and one place above newly promoted Town.

Oops – what have I done? Hands on hips, Manchester United defender contemplates his own-goal that gave Town a 1–0 win at Portman Road in February 1969. John O'Rourke and Chris Barnard are the celebrating Ipswich players.

A few short months earlier, Alex Stepney and Nobby Stiles had been celebrating winning the European Cup. Famously, it was Stepney's point-blank save from Benfica's star striker Eusebio that had kept United in the game. Here are the celebrated duo, retrieving the ball from the back of their net after Tony Dunne's own-goal had gifted Town victory in February 1969.

Town have just beaten mighty Manchester United 1–0 at Portman Road, and the youngsters in the crowd cannot contain their excitement.

Those were the days – when winters really were winters! Here is the Town squad braving the snow, ice and freezing temperatures, training on the practice pitch at Portman Road in February 1969. There were no nice warm gyms in those days.

One of Town's best results in their first season back in the First Division was this 2–0 win at Arsenal in February 1969. Town's scorers were O'Rourke and Crawford. For the striker nicknamed 'Jungle Boy' it was his 227th and final goal for Town. He moved to Charlton shortly afterwards. In this picture, Arsenal 'keeper Bob Wilson gathers the ball safely under pressure from Ipswich substitute Bobby Hunt. Crawford and Arsenal's Ian Ure (number five) look on.

John O'Rourke, in the middle of the picture, was Town's goalscorer in a 1–1 draw against Wolves at Molineux in March 1969.

Farewell to a legend – Ray Crawford pictured in his last game in Town's colours, away at Wolves in March 1969. The game ended 1–1, but Crawford was not on the scoresheet. His strike partner John O'Rourke scored Town's goal, so Crawford departed having scored 227 goals in 353 games for Ipswich in two spells. How he won only two England caps, only Walter Winterbottom and Alf Ramsey will know.

The King is dead, long live the King! Ray Crawford has departed for Wolves, and youngster Ron Wigg has taken the number-nine shirt. It all started well for him, with this goal in a 2–1 win over Manchester City in March 1969. One young fan seems to have got rather carried away. Sadly for our Ron, it was not to last.

This certainly does not look a like a contender for goal of the season, but they all count. Ron Wigg has just scored the winner for Town against Sunderland in April 1969. Youngster Wigg was promoted from the reserves after Ray Crawford left for Charlton, but he never really commanded a first-team place. In all honesty, it would be some seasons before Town found themselves another prolific goalscorer to replace Crawford.

David Best punches clear under extreme pressure in this game against Stoke at the Victoria Ground in April 1969. Mick Mills (on the line), Derek Jefferson and Peter Morris are the Town defenders. Stoke won 2–1. John O'Rourke, pictured in the background, scored the consolation goal for Ipswich.

1969–70: A great escape

Robson's first full season was a struggle, especially when it came to goalscoring. Crawford had departed during the previous season, and then O'Rourke left for Coventry early in 1969–70. Colin Viljoen ended up as top scorer on the grand total of six. Town were in serious danger of relegation until Robson pulled off a double masterstroke, with the signings of experienced pair Jimmy Robertson, from Arsenal, and Frank Clarke, from Queen's Park Rangers.

Robertson and Clarke inspired Town to a successful end-of-season run-in, during which they managed four wins in their last seven games, including a vital 2–0 win over relegation rivals Sunderland, in which Trevor Whymark scored his first senior goal for Town. Ipswich eventually finished five points clear of the drop.

Division One final position: 18th.

FA Cup: Third Round.

League Cup: Third Round.

The first-team squad for Bobby Robson's first full season in charge at Portman Road, pictured in August 1969. Standing, left to right: Mick Lambert, Derek Jefferson, Charlie Woods, Ron Wigg, David Best, John O'Rourke, Mick McNeil, Bobby Bell. Seated, left to right: Mick Mills, Colin Harper, Peter Morris, Billy Baxter, Tommy Carroll, Ian Collard, Clive Woods. Front: Steve Stacey and Frank Brogan. Of the 17 pictured here, only Mick Mills, Clive Woods and to a lesser extent Mick Lambert went on to play major roles in the Robson 'Glory Years' that were to follow.

It was a hot July day in 1969, and the Town players do not look best pleased to be back in pre-season training. Mick Mills, David Best and Colin Harper are among those doing laps of the practice pitch.

Behind you! Peter Morris does not realise that notorious Chelsea hardman Ron 'Chopper' Harris is in the vicinity. This is Ipswich playing at Chelsea in August 1969, when they lost 1–0 to an Ian Hutchinson goal. Tommy Carroll and 'keeper David Best are also on hand to deal with the cross.

Colin Viljoen shoots during Town's 1–0 defeat at Chelsea in August 1969. John Dempsey, he of the dodgy comb-over, is closing in from the left.

Town striker Ron Wigg challenges Coventry hard-man defender George Curtis in the game at Portman Road in August 1969. Coventry won 1–0 in a game which set the tone for a difficult season for Ipswich. They finished fifth from bottom of Division One, with a lack of goals being their biggest problem. Colin Viljoen was top scorer with six.

Coventry 'keeper Bill Glazier punches the ball away under pressure from Town's number six, Derek 'Chopper' Jefferson. The nickname came from his 'whole-hearted' style of play. Town lost this game 1–0, to a goal from diminutive Coventry midfielder Willie Carr. The defeat was part of a dreadful start to Town's second season back in Division One. After seven League games, they had only one point. With Crawford gone, and O'Rourke (number 10 in this picture) soon to join Coventry, goals were at a premium. Town still somehow managed to escape the drop.

Losing 1–0 to Coventry at home was just one of a series of poor results for Ipswich at the beginning of the 1969–70 season. John O'Rourke is seen here, battling against the Coventry defence. Ironically, he was to join the Sky Blues only a few weeks later.

The illustrious names of Greaves, Gilzean and Mullery were all on the Spurs scoresheet as the home team beat Ipswich 3–2 at White Hart Lane in August 1969. Ron Wigg and Colin Viljoen scored for Town. In this picture, Wigg gets in a shot despite the best efforts of Alan Mullery.

Goalkeeper David Best and centre-halves Bill Baxter and Derek Jefferson join forces to thwart this Spurs attack in August 1969. Mind you, they have a task and a half on their hands – the Spurs number eight is no less than a certain Jimmy Greaves. His striker partner Alan Gilzean is also in the thick of the action.

Goalkeeper Iam McFaul and a tumbling Bobby Moncur frustrate Town striker Ron Wigg at Portman Road in September 1969. Wigg and John O'Rourke were on target in a 2–0 win against Newcastle.

Ron Wigg celebrates scoring Town's second goal in a 2–0 home win against Newcastle, holders of the Inter City Fairs Cup, in September 1969. The Newcastle players look particularly miserable. Perhaps they realise that 40 years later the club would still be looking for its next taste of glory?

John O'Rourke pictured in action against West Bromwich Albion at the Hawthorns in September 1969. The game ended 2–2, with O'Rourke one of Town's scorers. The other Ipswich goal came from Ian Collard, who had only joined from West Brom a few weeks earlier. Midfielder Collard had played in West Brom's 1968 FA Cup victory over Everton – a game made famous by Jeff Astle's winning goal. Collard joined Town in a deal which saw crowd favourite Danny Hegan going the other way.

Mick McNeil, Colin Harper and Bill Baxter seem to be ganging up on Suffolk-born Arsenal player Jon Sammels in this game at Highbury in October 1969. Ian Collard seems happy to let them get on with it. The match ended goalless.

An early example of Mick Mills's shooting prowess on display against Sheffield Wednesday at Portman Road in October 1969. Even Millsy's biggest fans will admit that shooting was not the strongest part of his game. Not surprisingly, this effort did not result in a goal; however, Town did win the game, thanks to a Mick Lambert strike.

Striker Mick Hill flattered to deceive during his time with Ipswich Town. Despite some memorable goals, his scoring record was poor. Here is one of his best games, against Crystal Palace in November 1969. Hill scored both goals in a 2–0 win.

Legend in the snow. Bobby Moore looks on as his 'keeper Ferguson catches the ball under pressure from Mick Hill. It was November 1969, and a West Ham team containing three World Cup-winning legends – Moore, Hurst and Peters – have come to Portman Road. Town sneaked a 1–0 win, thanks to that rarest of treats – a Mick Mills goal.

Action from a six-goal thriller at Stoke in November 1969. Mick Lambert, Ian Collard and Colin Viljoen (penalty) scored Town's goals in a 3–3 draw at the Victoria Ground. It was one of Viljoen's six goals that season, making him leading scorer in a campaign that was one long goal drought. This game was featured on *Match of the Day* – a rare appearance for Ipswich in those days.

You would not find professional footballers these days playing two games in 24 hours, but that is what they did way back then. Town lined up at Coventry on Boxing Day 1969, and then again at home to Spurs a day later. In the picture, Mick Hill is thwarted this time by Spurs defender Phil Beal and legendary 'keeper Pat Jennings. But Welsh international Hill had the last laugh, scoring one of Town's goals in a 2–0 win over the Londoners at Portman Road. The other goal was a rare strike from Charlie Woods. Jimmy Greaves was playing one of his last games for Tottenham.

A rare sight – a goal from Charlie Woods. This was one of Town's goals in a 2–0 win over Spurs two days after Christmas in 1969. It was not the most thrilling of seasons – Town narrowly staved off relegation in a dour campaign which saw them fail to find the net in no fewer than 17 League games.

It looks like battle scene, but it is really only a football match. This is Town at Coventry in December 1969, when they slumped to a 3–1 defeat. Colin Harper is the Town player lying prone after clashing with former teammate John O'Rourke. It was not a great day for Harper all round – he also scored an own-goal.